This book is dedicated to all my family and friends who supported me, and it is also dedicated to readers who choose and take the time to read it with attention.

CONTENTS

INTRODUCTION

With the expansion of AI, the internet of things, machine learning, deep learning, VR, and AR, all aspects of our lives and day-to-day lives become tracked, clouded, evaluated, and shared.

Our personal information, especially sensitive ones or what we now call big data, is used by algorithms like input and sold to marketers or organizations as human capital markets.

Reality is mixed with virtual one and augmented one, that we could not separate them which is the picture of today future and more.

We are tracked permanently by the big tech, and they profile us with all our connections to social media, our phones, our IoT, our chipped cards, our health records.

METAVERSE SQUARE highlights every aspect of our daily life in the light of the development of artificial intelligence and robotics and let you dive into the universe of the metaverse developed by the giants of the web and in which virtual reality, crypto, gaming are the keywords; the phenomenon has experienced an unprecedented boom in recent months and brings with it concepts now well known in the ecosystem.

METAVERSE SQUARE did not pretend to master any topics discussed but give you an insight into a large picture of what we live and what we expect to live many hours from now.

METAVERSE SQUARE tries to make it easier for you to understand all topics related to metaverse world, and its impact on the era in which they live.

CHAPTER 1: ARTIFICIAL INTELLIGENCE

Artificial Intelligence

Artificial intelligence is a field of computing and is also a concept that is difficult to define completely exactly due to its very complexity.

In the broad sense, the term AI designates systems in the domain of pure science and systems already operational in the capacity to perform very complex tasks.

It contributes to nurturing purely speculative fears that would remain anecdotal if they did not disturb the measurement of real issues, such as the impact on fundamental rights of grounded decision-making processes; on mathematical models, and therefore difficult to develop regulatory frameworks.

Many people are unaware of what artificial intelligence is and how it works; Doctors use it for diagnostics and plan treatments, market forecasting is more efficient with AI, and Google's search algorithms are also more dynamic.

AI sits behind every assistant such as Siri, helps cars be self-sufficient, or can help select new employees; laws are already being created with the help of artificial intelligence, research has made many advances in recent years about subdivisions.

The faculties that are part of intelligence and are controversial in humans are even more so when applied to machines

This simulation approach aims to reproduce the same functionalities as the brain;

Create the result do not matter, is what people know about artificial intelligence.

We can speak to him about an intelligent system; artificial intelligence is divided into two categories: strong AI and weak AI.

AI is a young discipline of sixty years old, which brings together sciences, theories, and techniques and whose goal is to make people imitate a machine the cognitive abilities of a human being.

Specialists generally prefer to use the exact name of the technologies implemented and are sometimes reluctant to use the term intelligence because the results, although extraordinary in certain areas, remain modest given the ambitions maintained; and its purpose is to enable computers to think and act like human beings.

Management systems and advanced AI algorithms

Artificial intelligence needs many data and a high processing capacity to get as close to human behavior.

AI Uses

AI is present in our daily lives; it is used by the fraud detection services of financial institutions for forecasting purchase intentions and in interactions with online customer services; here are some:

Fraud detection

In the finance industry, artificial intelligence is used in two ways, Apps that score credit applications use AI to assess consumers' creditworthiness; more advanced AI engines are responsible for monitoring and detecting fraudulent payments made by credit cards in real-time.

Virtual Customer Service

Call centers use an SCV to predict and respond to customer requests without human intervention. Speech recognition and a human dialogue simulator are the first interaction points with customer service; more complex requests require human intervention.

When an Internet user opens a dialogue window on a web page (chatbot), his interlocutor is often a computer running a form of specialized AI.

If the chatbot fails to interpret the question or resolve the issue, a human agent takes over; these interpretation failures are sent to the machine learning system to improve future interactions of the AI application.

Increasingly diverse: understanding natural language, visual recognition, robotics, autonomous system, Machine Learning.

AI challenges

According to some experts, AI researchers, and pioneers of deep learning, the ambition to succeed in imitating human cognition would require discoveries in fundamental research and not a simple evolution of current technologies; machine learning, such technologies, which are essentially mathematical and statistical, are not able to act by intuition or quickly model their environment.

Societal, ethical, and fundamental rights impacts are therefore not to be constructed by fearing that machine learning will cause an artificial form of consciousness to emerge within 10 or 20 years, but preventing bias, discrimination, and harm to life; privacy, freedom of expression or conscience, even life itself with the autonomous weapons resulting from a conception of society reducing it to a mathematical model.

Strong AI

The definition of strong artificial intelligence is intelligence that can fully replace the scope of human intelligence in all its complexity; this universal man-machine approach has been around cognitive, psychomotor, social, and emotional bits of intelligence; most contemporary AI programs rely primarily on cognitive intelligence: logic, organization, problem-solving, autonomy, or forming.

Self-driving cars, medical diagnostics, and search algorithms.

Research has made tremendous progress in weak AI; developing intelligent systems in specific areas has proven more practical and ethical than researching super-intelligence.

The application areas are very large but are particularly successful in medicine, finance, transportation, marketing, and of course, the Internet; one can already foresee that artificial intelligence technology of this type.

Symbolic AI

Symbolic AI is our classic approach, but also other logical disciplines, such as chess; symbolic AI operates by strict rules and can solve extremely complex problems through the development of computing capabilities.

Yet the limits of symbolic AI are increasingly evident; it does not matter, therefore, the degree of complexity of the expert system because symbolic artificial intelligence acquiring independent knowledge.

The mid-1970s began the AI winter, a difficult time for artificial intelligence, which suffered many independently and progressing; research developed around artificial neural intelligence.

Neural AI

Geoffrey Hinton and two of his colleagues, in 1986, developed the concept of artificial neural, they developed back propagation of the gradient even further; this laid the foundation for deep learning, used today by almost all artificial intelligence technologies.

This learning algorithm allows deep neural networks to learn and develop independently continuously; this represents a great challenge that the symbolic IA could not meet.

Therefore, Neuronal AI is distinguished from the principles of symbolic representation of knowledge. With human intelligence, knowledge is segmented into small functioning units, artificial neurons linked to ever-growing groups.

Neural AI intends to mimic the brain's functioning as precisely as possible in the field of robotics, experiences that AI itself generates ever-growing knowledge; this is where the major innovation lies: although training itself takes much time, it allows the machine to learn on its own in the longer term.

We sometimes speak of learning machines; this makes neural AI-based machines highly dynamic and adaptable systems that humans sometimes no longer fully understand.

An infinite number of artificial neurons are arranged on top of each other in a system of layers, and simulated cables connect them.

Deep neural networks, that is, those that communicate with more than two layers, work; the middle layers are arranged hierarchically on top of the others; in some systems, information about millions of connections is communicated upwards.

The top layer acts as a sensor, which absorbs data into the system, whether through the network according to specific patterns and then compared to the previous information: the upper layer constantly feeds and trains the entire system.

The lower layer acts as the production layer but has fewer neurons since it has one per classified category; the production layer tells the user neural network results and can recognize a new photo of a previously unknown cat.

There are three basic methods used for neural network training: supervised, unsupervised, or over-training; these methods regulate how the sensor is directed towards the desired output.

Innovation is based on the incredible exploits of systems capable of learning independently, whether learning a language, driving, or recognizing Handwriting.

AI Opportunities and risks

Artificial intelligence elicits widely varying reactions from blind optimists into the future to outright rejection of technical progress.

AI advantages

Advancement highlights the benefits of artificial intelligence in the following areas:

Improving working conditions

It has concluded their livelihood securely through work alone.

Comfort

AI advocates also see an opportunity to improve daily comfort through numerous innovations; this applies to self-driving cars or intelligent translation software, representing less workload for users.

Outstanding performance

Artificial intelligence also has huge can help identify the characteristics of a trial faster and reach impartial judgments more easily.

Economic benefits

A study by Merrill Lynch estimates that by 2020 the artificial intelligence industry will see an increase of $ 150 billion; AI is, therefore, a key sector for IT and neighboring industries and increasing income in general.

Futuristic projects

AI fuels the desire for human exploration; it is already developed to search for new sources of oil or control robots on Mars; likely, advancing research on space exploration will also help advance research on artificial intelligence.

AI dangers

Inferiority of Humanity

One of the possible risks that science fiction has already raised in the development of super-intelligence; we mean intelligence capable of self-development and freedom from humanity.

The relations between humans and such robots could become

problematic, these super-intelligences overtake and dominate humans; however, researchers believe it is almost impossible to set will become so proficient in their field that they develop self-sufficient activities that could be harmful to humankind, surrounding super-intelligence.

Dependence on technology

Critics of artificial intelligence also see it as a loss of human power, which would increasingly depend on technological systems; in the medical field, humans are becoming objects increasingly observed and monitored by machines, according to artificial intelligence opponents.

There is a risk of losing our privacy and our self-determination; these concerns apply to medicine and artificial intelligence-assisted video surveillance or intelligent algorithms on the Internet.

Data protection and distribution of powers

Intelligent algorithms can process increasing amounts of data with increasing efficiency, but the processing of data power does not only concern AI but all areas of IT in the digital age.

Filter bubbles and selective perception

Internet activist warns of another danger of artificial intelligence, a concept called filter bubbles, and his theory is that algorithms take more and more importance and distract are likely to click on.

Following their convictions, it is the opinion of experts that algorithms thus contribute to increasing an ideological distance between individuals.

A Microsoft study, published in 2016, investigates the disparity of information received by different users through filter bubbles; the results, however, play down the role of artificial intelligence: the study shows that similar problems exist in mainstream journalism and that the impact of new technologies has yet to be full.

Vacancies; critics of AI fear it will make humans increasingly re-
dundant due to the development of robots specializing in cleaning, personal care, and autonomous transportation systems; robots specializing in the care of the elderly are particularly controversial, as they are accused of providing cold, inhuman care,
especially special attention.

Discriminant Algorithm

Microsoft's chatbot stay imitated racist speech in no time, security technologies have classified black neighborhoods as problem
areas, and job platforms offer better-paid offers for men.

The problem is well known, and the British Standards Institute
has published an updated version of its ethical guidelines for robots; however, it is difficult to implement these instructions sys-
tematically since each artificial intelligence learns on its own in
contact with its ever-present racism and sexism.

AI in the digital world

It should be noted that AI is barely visible on the Internet;
many companies avoid using the term, even though AI powers
their products; without necessarily realizing it may somehow
be reluctant to use it; in addition, smart, the easy transitions
between the steps; yet there are many other areas of the web in
which AI technologies play a key role: from software to active algorithms, the list goes on.

Google dominates this market with its innovations, apparently
two to three years ahead of competing companies, so:

What is the role played by artificial intelligence in the famous
algorithms?

What are its effects on online marketing?

Techniques and fields of application

Machine learning

Machine learning refers to, and machine learning uses both symbolic and neural artificial intelligence.

Deep learning

Which only involves artificial neural networks; this forms the basis of most AI applications, speech recognition and sound recognition.

Social computing

It allows the analysis of much online content; helps develop artificial social agents.

Opinion Analysis

This term refers to the methods used on the web to collect opinions, and opinion analysis also makes it possible to deal with customer inquiries in an automatic or personalized manner.

Customer service and digital assistance

Artificial intelligence plays a key role in this industry, especially thanks to voice recognition programs, whose importance in search rankings is constantly increasing.

Web crawlers

These crawlers, also called crawlers, are used by search engines to scan the web for information and create indexes; web robots learn from examples and are therefore able to draw relevant conclusions.

Computerized vision system

Computerized vision, especially such as is not looking at the lens.

Virtual gamers and bots

Gamers that behave more like humans; Bots, and social bots, in particular, were developed to simulate human activity on the web.

Group simulation

Artificial intelligence can predict complex human behavior patterns in groups; this technique is used for video games and security technologies or the analysis of viral dynamics.

Research programs, algorithms, and initiatives

Rank Brain

It is an intelligent algorithm from Google, which was originally developed to better understand long and unknown queries; in 2015, Google reported that Rank Brain was ranked third out of 200 search items in Google search; this is why Rank Brain has such a big influence on SEO.

Deep Mind

it is a company bought by Google in 2014, which has developed several artificial intelligence technologies, its developments, including Rank Brain, are integrated into several Google applications and algorithms.

One of Deep Mind's AIs self-trained her memory by practicing old Atari games; the company also developed Alpha Go, the program that brought the game of Go to a new level of perfection; from a technical point of view, Deep Mind not only relies on a neural network but also has a short-term memory system, which makes it possible to simulate the mechanisms of human memory even better.

Siri, Alexa, Cortana

The artificial bits of intelligence of voice assistants from Apple, Amazon, and Microsoft o ask questions and naturally answer them.

In 2011, he participated in the Jeopardy and had the opportunity to demonstrate his gathered data from insured persons and study their medical history.

In 2016, this artificial intelligence autonomously created the trailer for the movie Morgan from a hundred trailers that fed the algorithm.

Cleverbot

The instant communication program learns by communicating with humans; this open-source chat program was classified as human after scoring 59.3% on the Turing test.

Tensor Flow

Sensor Flow has since been used for various Google products, including voice recognition, Gmail, and Google search.

AI effects on SEO

Deep Mind in 2014, Google started a trend and showed that its search algorithm was increasingly geared towards artificial intelligence.

The intelligent Rank Brain algorithm is the one that most influences Google's artificial intelligence initiatives, very effective at.

Rank Brain's specialty is converting text queries into mathematical entities so as better to understand the intent behind the formulation of the query; however, it is not clear how exactly artificial intelligence works, f artificial intelligence in Google search.

They are already moving from mobile-first to Artificial Intelligence First.

They want to build a personal Google for every user, a personalized Google, and the perfect individualization of online search.

Rank Brain's artificial intelligence categorizes search queries, transforming available data into hypotheses and generalizations that it applies to the respective data, as the algorithm is constantly fed with new data and pin down.

Artificial intelligence daily acquires its knowledge from the quality of websites, which it applies to future rankings, thanks to the experiences and reports of users.

It is essential to keep in mind that user signals are of paramount importance, it is no longer just about the number of clicks, but also how much time users spend on; internet users click on an element in proportion to the number of times this element is displayed.

Semantics before keywords

Originally, Rank Brain was developed to understand better long and novel queries; as a result, Google interprets each of the requests every day, which allows it to understand.

Google can see if the user is happy or not

Google evaluates user signals and ranks websites based on their quality, much more accurately than pre-Rank Brain algorithms; it is, therefore, more than ever essential to develop the user-friendliness of Internet sites, intelligible texts, and a judicious link building constitute the bases of usability.

Both users and artificial intelligence must easily understand view and load; in short, content is essential, but it must be paired with a perfect technique for maximized SEO results.

Bet on versatile online marketing

The bigger a business, the more investment is needed in online marketing by surrounding yourself with SEO, social media, and user-friendliness specialists; to best adapt to advances in artificial intelligence, all these actors must work together.

While rankings are becoming more flexible, the good news is that search engine optimization is changing relatively.

It should be noted that in 2016, five digital giants from Silicon Valley came together to work together on research on artificial intelligence, this news immediately alarmed data protection consumers because these companies hold much information about their users, but this cooperation is above all designed to develop common ethical recommendations regarding the use of artificial intelligence.

It is undeniable that common rules must be established in this area; directing the progress of artificial intelligence into proper channels should become one of the essential tasks of communication and the media in the years to come.

The applications that enable machine learning, the basis of artificial intelligence, are supported by artificial neural networks.

Bottleneck

Harness the light, and the network can perform 10 trillion operations per second, and overlap; this type of network is used particularly for face recognition and computer image applications and speech, accelerating the acquisition of an image in convolution stages.

A breakthrough for autonomous vehicles

A convolutional neural network has been developed, and it is capable of processing images up to 250,000 pixels, at exciting prospects in big data learning for real-time and very high-speed.

The devices were developed based on recurrent neural network architectures; these networks, inspired by brain circuits, have short-term memory essential for processing dynamic data sequences.

A fundamental aspect of this system is that the number of neurons needed in the network is reduced thanks to time-division multiplexing; this allows to creation of virtual neurons from a single physical neuron, and the number of virtual neurons created varies according to the applications.

This technique has the advantage of reducing the complexity and number of components required compared to other artificial neural networks during their design, and the photonic recurrent neural networks studied have the potential to perform a wider range of complex and time-consuming learning tasks such as speech recognition, financial forecasting, and medical diagnosis.

AI and neurons merge

All over the world, laboratories are in turmoil to try to erase the faults of artificial intelligence algorithms and increase their capacities tenfold.

Improve neuronal plasticity

The human brain is constantly changing the connections between its neurons; they are made, broken down, weakened, and strengthened; this allows him to repair himself after an injury, learn, or forget.

This plasticity is greatest at the early stages of life, a critical period during as a child's mind develops, with comparable plasticity?

Nothing is acquired, but the way is open, including those who work closely with industrial applications of AI.

Thus, some researchers working in Uber's research and development units and their work focused on autonomous driving software are helping to prepare the next generation of AI by experimenting with new algorithms equipped with plasticity.

Or algorithms with the ability, after training, to partially reconfigure the connections between their artificial neurons to accomplish a slightly different task; this plasticity helps them to learn in a way.

The level of plasticity, to help machines soften their learning capacities, is strongly inspired by the maturation processes observed in childhood in the heart of the human brain.

At birth, a newborn baby already has around 100 billion neurons, only half of these neurons are then connected, but, minute after minute, about 2 million connections will be set up, under the influence of genetic factors and interactions with the environment.

To endow a machine with even a modest fraction of this formidable plasticity, over time and not only during an initial training carried out for a specific purpose, but it is also to give it chances of power to adapt its behavior to a complex and changing environment.

Studies have shown that before the age of 2, children are already sensitive to syntax; they judge sentences where verbs and nouns are incorrectly placed to be abnormal, and newborns as young as 30 hours old already have an abstract representation of the number.

Would it be possible not to base the capabilities of AI solely on acquired knowledge, but to endow them with innate skills, thanks to a computer code that would offer them essential skills, even before exposing them to the immense reservoirs of data that today constitutes their only baggage, this is one of the challenges ahead.

Elon Musk AI project

Elon Musk, CEO of Tesla and Space X, is also leading a wacky and exciting project, the development of a neural technology company called Neuralink.

He co-founded Neuralink in 2016, and the company remained relatively secretive until 2017 when the Wall Street Journal announced he created it to merge the computer with the human brain.

The development of brain chips is a curious side business for a man who simultaneously runs Tesla, his space exploration company Space X, and The Boring Company, through which he hopes to dig underground transportation networks for cities.

But Neuralink focuses on one of Musk's main fears, artificial intelligence; the entrepreneur has often expressed his fears that AI one day eclipses the human species.

He founded a multi-purpose research organization called OpenAI, but Neuralink has a much more tangible and futuristic goal of making devices powered by artificial intelligence interact with people's brains.

In July, Neuralink executives and Elon Musk presented the advancements in technology developed by the company; the big news was the revelation of a tiny microchip that could, theoretically, be implanted behind a person's ear with tiny wires containing electrodes extending into the brain.

The concept is not new; scientists have already created devices that can both interpret brain activity and stimulate neurons in the brain; in addition to treating neural diseases like Parkinson's, he hopes Neuralink could one day facilitate symbiosis between humans and AI; he also enthusiastically announced that the company had succeeded in getting begin testing in humans.

Business Insider US spoke to two neuroscientists springing from science and theory, and there are some strong arguments and some very real aspects to consider in this announcement.

The wires of the device proposed by Neuralink and that the company uses could, according to Alex Hires, advances the subject because of their flexibility; the fact that they are using these flexible wires is an important innovation, especially if they are trying to reach consumers;

The stiff wires in the brain cause much damage because the brain can move around them, and a living brain is very soft, much softer than specimens you might have seen in jars that have been stiffened with formalin.

It is much sweeter than jelly; Soft threads like those described by Neuralink might be a better solution for any device that is supposed to spend a long time in someone's brain because they are less likely to ignite or damage tissue.

But it is recent enough that we do not know if these wires could last longer than two years; the technology has only been out for, and they break.

A polymer commonly used in this field; the electrodes themselves are made of gold, called research-level technology, rather than technology already ready to be put into people's brains.

A sewing machine instead of a surgeon

A big problem with flexible wires is that they can be difficult to thread through the brain, and Neuralink has invented something entirely new for this, and the probes would be inserted into the brain by a device similar to the sewing machine, which would use a stiff needle to push threads about 1 millimeter into the brain's outer surface, or cortex.

The idea for this sewing machine is brand new, it is an important innovation; we had to insert similar devices into the brains of mice manually; it was very difficult.

It is with a feature of the machine that could neutralize the usual sloshing of the brain, there is the breathing, the beating of the heart, and those two factors can make the brain move a bit; this feature is called in-line motion correction.

A super-powerful chip that translates brain activity

The latest weapon in Neuralink's arsenal is the chip that will interpret the brain activity picked up by the electrodes; the problem with the electrical signals that come out of the brain is that they are very small, and the more they travel a thin wire, the more they will be distorted by noise because there is always electrical noise; in the world around us.

From what they revealed in their white paper, this chip goes way beyond state of the art, and it will allow you to record from more places; with greater precision, it is a bit like upgrading your TV from standard definition to high definition.

The most exciting thing about Neuralink is not that any of these three technologies have been brought together; all of these different aspects now and it is nice to see them together in one device.

While Elon Musk is keen to tout the future fusion of artificial intelligence and human consciousness, Alex Hires and Rylie Green are more enthusiastic about the short-term benefits that mind control for a robotic arm for paralyzed patients with lock-in syndrome could use to give them.

Electrons in Neuralink will not necessarily stimulate the right neurons to generate this sensation due to the brain's adaptability.

Alex Hires and Rylie Green were more skeptical of Elon Musk's goal that Neuralink will one day facilitate the increase in human consciousness through artificial intelligence; however, to get to a level of integration through AI, that is where kind of goes to a great, ambitious country, but it is hard to predict how the technology will change in twenty years.

Neuralink's biggest hurdle comes long before the company tries to put AI in anyone's brain; getting either of these devices into your brain is a very, very high-risk surgery.

CHAPTER 2: MACHINE LEARNING

Machine Learning

Still confusing for many people, Machine Learning is a modern science for discovering repetitions in one or more data streams and making predictions based on statistics.

Clearly, Machine Learning is based on data mining, allowing pattern recognition to provide predictive analyzes.

The first machine learning algorithms are not new, as some were designed as early as 1950, the best known of which is the Perceptron, its precise definition is still confusing, and pattern recognition and predictive analyzes.

History

Robots and automatons have been a source of interest for several centuries, Writers of the Romantic period were already dealing with artificial intelligence; approach; the technology is now agile enough to access and analyze colossal data sets; companies from all industries are joining Google and Amazon to implement AI solutions for their businesses.

An example of applied machine learning: MetLife, one of the world's leading corporate insurers, uses this technique and big data to optimize its business; speech recognition enabled him to improve the tracking of accidents and better measure their consequences; complaints handling is now better supported as the complaint models have been enriched using unstructured data that can be analyzed through this technology.

Another example, this technique makes it possible to learn the habits of the occupants of a home, designers of connected objects, including thermostats, can analyze the temperature of the home to understand the presence and absence of occupants to turn off the heat and turn it back on a few minutes before their return.

Machine learning and big data

Without Big Data, which as a reminder is a concept for storing an indescribable amount of data on a digital basis, artificial intelligence (AI) and machine learning would be nothing.

Indeed, data is the indispensable tool for artificial intelligence to understand and learn the way human intelligence analyzes situations; it is, therefore, Big Data that enables the automation of data processing by allowing the acceleration of the learning curve of computers relying on Machine Learning.

Now, artificial intelligence is fully capable of learning without the help of a human that is to say autonomously, Google's Deep-Mind algorithm, which has taught itself to play around 40 Atari videos before the arrival of Big Data, due to insufficient data sets.

Nowadays, large datasets are accessible at any time, and in real-time, in particular, this context allows artificial intelligence and machine learning to take a holistic approach to data processing, with the technology now advanced enough to access and analyze colossal amounts of information; as a result, many companies are joining Google and Amazon to implement AI solutions in their companies.

An example of AI using Machine Learning: connected objects, they can learn the habits of the occupants of a home in order to perform one or more tasks when they want them; this is how, thermostats can analyze the temperature of a home in order to detect the presence or absence of its occupants and turn the heating off or on again accordingly.

Performing predictive analyses involves exploiting data from Big Data and processed by statistical algorithms and Machine Learning techniques to predict probabilities based on the past.

Predictive analyses are carried out from several disciplines and technologies such as data mining, statistical analyses, predictive modeling, and of course, Machine learning to allow companies to predict tomorrow's financial trends and results.

These predictive analyzes are the ultimate goal of machine learning; they help extract actionable insights from large data sets, giving businesses the ability to make better strategic decisions in line with their goals.

Next levels of data analysis, with IT systems now able to continuously learn from data captured by businesses in order to predict consumer needs intelligently, trends futures of a particular market, and much more; such a level of expertise can only be achieved by cognitive computer systems capable of understanding unstructured data, reasoning in order to extract predictive analyzes refined as each interaction occurs.

Find it! In the past, computer scientists looked for patterns and trends in data; when the amount of data is very large, this search can be difficult, but computers speed up this process.

World data

The short answer is, there are a lot! People generate large amounts of data using the Internet and other communication tools, these large amounts of data are often referred to as big data, scientists have had to invent ever more powerful systems to process all this data.

Cloud computing is a good example; this system was developed because ordinary computers could no longer efficiently process the huge volume of data received.

These large amounts of data have changed the relationship between humans and computers; in the past, humans used computers to organize and represent data, but it was humans who made the data meaningful; today's machines help us figure out how to understand and explain vast amounts of data, this is what we call machine learning.

ML Uses

Involving large volumes of data almost anywhere; companies were the first to take advantage of machine learning because they could invest in these technologies; machine learning today costs less and is easier to access; many machine learning programs are shared online as open source.

The possibilities of machine learning are endless, and we are only just beginning to learn how to use this powerful tool.

ML Common types and algorithms

Regression

In its simplest form, it is a straight line that crosses a set of data points; it shows the supposed linear relationship between two variables so that from one variable it is possible to deduce the next; this method also allows you to calculate error values that allow you to specify a confidence interval for the results.

It is thus easily possible to pass from linear regression to a multiple or polynomial linear regression; with these methods, adjustments are usually made using the least-squares approximation to minimize the distance of the curve from the data points.

Another often used adjustment technique is logistic regression, it fits the data to a sigmoid curve (S-shaped) and outputs a probability (0 to 1); as a probability, this is a two-class problem; basically, it is a statistical relation of the compactness of a class in characteristic space and its proximity to other classes.

Edge regression

Unlike the regression methods mentioned above, this method is suitable for situations where no perfect information is available what is called an ill-posed problem; compared to neural networks, only a small amount of system training data is available here, from this data, no satisfactory line or curve is obtained that classifies the data adequately; applying any of the above methods would lead to over-learning or under-learning.

This regularization is known as the Tikhonov matrix, to find the Tikhonov matrix, it is we can assume, for example, that the data d that they contain enough deviations to be able to determine approximately the mean deviation and the standard deviation, or that all the variables have the same standard deviation.

The CVB Polimago tool uses this type of algorithm: it is used as a tool for finding variable objects or as a classifier in case of discrepancies in the object classes, and it is, therefore, necessary to generalize; marginal cases are useful for training in the algorithm to separate classes from each other.

Decision tree

A decision tree looks like a small neural network except that decision nodes are generally known; the CVB Minos tool is one example, with each decision node representing a binary decision, this leads to a very fast classifier since it is possible to exclude 50% of the possible results for each decision, CVB Minos thus makes it possible to be very fast in the tasks of optical character recognition (OCR) and research based on the learned characteristics.

Support vector machine

Characteristics whose coordinates are called "support vectors; in the case of a two-class problem, the SVM separates the two groups of points by defining a dividing line with maximum margin, that is, with a maximum distance between the line and the nearest points; the SVM configuration defines the type of line - linear, polynomial, logarithmic.

The following graphics show that groups of points can be separated from each other with lines of different types; by setting limits to the authorized results, the characteristics of the solution can change.

Naive Bayesian Classifier

The term "Bayesian" refers to probability. A class has several unrelated properties, and a value likely relates to an ideal set of values for a given class; given a measure of color, a spherical object about 250 mm in radius could correspond to the class "soccer ball"; by changing any of these keywords, it is less likely that the object is a soccer ball.

Set K of nearest neighbors

A voting system uses the nearest neighbors within a feature space to determine the class to which a test property belongs; defining the K number is an extremely difficult part of the concept.

K-Averages

Compared to the K closest neighbors, this method "automatically" creates K data clusters: the clusters are fairly homogeneous even though they display large differences between themselves, it could be a simple iterative centroid problem; it is, however, entirely dependent on the properties measured - the resulting clusters may have no relation to human perception.

Random forest

It is an extension of the decision tree system; it only has several trees; here, the variable is related to an output variable; in more complex forests, the internal algorithms can be any of those mentioned elsewhere.

Therefore, it is a voting method based on the assumption that "most methods are correct most of the time"; unlike decision trees, random forests are less likely to over-adapt to training data.

Best types ML

Choosing the best machine learning technique depends on the problem at hand; it is also possible to combine solutions in order to obtain better results; we could use unsupervised machine learning supervised machine learning; finally, we could test its accuracy using input data from people with and without the disease in question.

Other thoughts on ML

The human brain works, but some things are still a mystery; this situation is very similar to machine learning; it is wonderful that machines do what we want them to do, but it is not enough.

If we do not know how they make their decisions, how do we know if they are fair and ethical? It is especially true when machine learning is used with data relevant to the general public; the ability to explain how machine learning works is called transparency or explainable artificial intelligence.

You might be wondering if humans are still needed since machines are capable of learning; the answer is yes, the quality of a machine learning algorithm depends on the quality of ensuring that the data used by machine learning models are accurate and relevant, we also need skilled people to ensure that these technologies are used wisely, and fairly many experts are working on it now, but more of them will be needed in the future.

Google's autonomous cars and Netflix's recommendations

Both use machine learning to make repeatable decisions, perform specific tasks, and adapt independently, with little or no human interaction.

To define machine learning in layman's terms, it is the science of making machines learn and act identically to humans, learning autonomously from real-world interactions and data sets.

Today, machine learning models interact with more complex data sets and learn through previously performed calculations and predictions to produce decisions and results.

ML applications

Machine Learning powers many popular modern services; one example is the recommendation engines used by Netflix, YouTube, Amazon, or Spotify.

The same goes for web search engines like Google or Baidu, and Social media feeds like Facebook and Twitter are machine learning, just like voice assistants like Siri and Alexa.

All of these platforms collect data about users.

ML systems also excel in games, AI has already surpassed humans at the game of go, chess, checkers, or shogi, and converting oral speech to the screen; and AI is very good at this, sometimes even better than human experts at detecting abnormalities.

Companies have automatically used machine learning to review candidate CVs; however, training data biases lead to discrimination in the business world.

It is a real problem, and Amazon, preferred to stop experimenting in this area; it is inferior for women and people of color.

Financial exchanges

Models and forecasts are the lifeblood of the stock market, and this is what makes stockbrokers rich; machine learning algorithms are used by some of the world's most prestigious trading companies to predict and execute high-volume, high-speed transactions.

Personalized marketing

And when we serve them better, we sell more; personalized Marketing uses machine learning algorithms to create a truly personalized customer experience that matches their past behavior, what they like and dislike, and location data, like where they prefer.

ML tools in businesses

Apple, Google, Facebook, and Microsoft are just a few of the tech giants leading the way in machine learning, last year in June, Apple released its Core ML API, designed to accelerate artificial intelligence on iPhone, and Microsoft's Azure cloud services now include an Emotion API, capable of detecting human emotions such as sadness, anger, happiness, disgust, and surprise.

These tools' competition and human error allow organizations to be more agile and responsive than ever.

In addition to using machine learning to improve processes and make data-driven decisions, organizations need to be able to manage their data security more effectively and in a way that does not slow down employees.

The solution is Dynamic Data Protection from Forcepoint, through human behavior analysis the time spent sorting through alerts and enabled your DevSecOps teams to be more proactive.

Deep Learning, a sub-domain of ML

itself is a sub-category of machine learning; the most common example of an application is visual recognition, an algorithm will be programmed to detect certain faces from images coming from a camera, depending on the database assigned.

It will be able to spot a wanted individual in a crowd, detect the satisfaction rate when leaving a store by detecting smiles, Etc., a set of, tone, expression of questioning, statement and words.

To do this, Deep Learning relies mainly on the reproduction of a neural network inspired by brain systems found in nature, and the developers decide according to the desired application what type of learning they will implement.

In this context, we speak of supervised learning, unsupervised learning in which the machine will feed on data not previously selected, semi-supervised, by reinforcement, or by transfer in which the algorithms will apply a learned solution in a situation never seen before.

However, this technique requires much data to practice and achieve sufficient success rates to be used, and a Data Lake is essential for perfecting the learning of Deep Learning algorithms; Deep learning also requires greater computing power to do its job.

Predictive Analytics Make Big Data meaningful modeling, and

Machine Learning to predict the future of companies, analytics help generates actionable insights from large data sets, enabling organizations to decide which direction to take next and deliver a better customer experience; with the increase in, such as Salesforce Einstein, many businesses can now use predictive analytics.

According to a study conducted by Bluewolf of 1,700 Salesforce customers, 75% of companies that increase their investments in analytics technologies are benefiting from it; 81% of these Salesforce product users believe that using predictive analytics is the most important initiative in their sales strategy, predictive analytics automate decision making, thereby increasing the profitability and productivity of a business.

Artificial Intelligence and machine learning represent the next level of data analysis; cognitive computing with data over time that goes unused, and it is about dark data.

Thanks to Machine Learning and different algorithms, it is possible to sort through these; afterward, a skilled and can be deleted; even though algorithms do not have the same capacity for discernment as humans, machine learning allows us to sort the data first; in this way, employees save valuable time before proceeding with the permanent deletion of obsolete data.

This technology is also useful for data integration in determining what kind of data to aggregate for their queries; analysts typically create a repository to place different data types from various sources to create an analytical data pool.

Finally, data learning helps organize data storage for better access; it is designed to simulate over the past five.

It is the concept we all think of when we talk about AI: machines or robots like C-3PO, Terminator, or Wall-E with the senses and intellect of human beings.

However, most of today's AI is narrow or weak, capable of performing very specific tasks. Some examples of weak AI: Apple

Siri, the recommendation for the next Netflix TV show, facial recognition on Facebook, all of these technologies present some facets of human intelligence, but how do they work? One of the answers is machine learning.

Machine learning is a device that uses algorithms to analyze data, learn from it, and then determine or predict something; in other words, the machine is trained using large amounts of data and algorithms that allow the system to learn to perform a task.

AM is good for facial, voice, and object recognition, translation, and many other tasks; unlike manual coding of software with specific instructions to accomplish a task, AM allows a system to recognize patterns on its own and make predictions.

Efficient, but not perfect, it still requires much human intervention, AM is used, among other things, I using thousands, or millions, of images to be able to identify traffic signs and determine if it is a "Stop," to then stop the vehicle; here again, efficient, but not perfect, especially on a snowy day when the panel is not perfectly visible or may be partially obstructed by a tree.

That involves a mathematical system inspired by the human brain: artificial neural networks; however, unlike our brains, where neurons are interconnected, these artificial neural networks have hidden layers, connections, and directions of data propagation.

Over the years, researchers have improved the concept through various techniques, such as adding multi-layers to make higher-level functionality accessible. The system can better predict the problem; we are talking about prediction here since the PA can be defined as a system of probabilities.

The system can provide statements, decisions, or predictions with a certain degree of certainty; the most popular example of AP is the detection and classification of a cat in an image; the system is trained using a huge data set and can transmit these results: it can be 91% sure that there is an animal in the image,

82% that it is a cat and 8% that it is a stuffed cat.

Then algorithms can be added or corrected, and even tell the machine that the decisions are correct or incorrect; AP has its limits: using more layers requires more computing power and more data to train; indeed, a large number of parameters must be understood by a learning algorithm.

After experiencing two periods of strong development, AI experienced a new boom in 2010 thanks to so-called machine learning algorithms, and two factors are at the origin of this new craze of processors of simple computer graphics cards to accelerate the calculation of algorithms.

Therefore, the current AI "revolution" does not come from the discovery of fundamental research but from the possibility of efficiently exploiting relatively old foundations, such as Bayesian inference or formal neurons.

Machine learning has operated a complete paradigm shift compared to the previous generation of AI, expert systems, with an approach intended as inductive: it will no longer be a question for a computer scientist to code the rules by hand but to let computers discover them by correlation and classification, based on a massive amount of data; in other words, the goal.

AI different views

Very concretely, in its learning phase, the machine will look for the links between data previously selected for a specific domain and categorize them; this model can then be used to solve questions such as: if it is 25 °, how many ice creams can I expect to sell in such and such a place?

Although some systems build models relatively autonomously, human intervention is still essential, whether it involves choosing the training data, identifying their possible biases, or, when possible, distinguishing among the correlations those that can be the cause of a phenomenon.

AI as we know it is weak Artificial Intelligence, as opposed to strong AI, which does not yet exist; today, machines reproduce human behavior, but without consciousness; later, their abilities could grow to the point of transforming into machines endowed with consciousness, sensitivity, and spirit.

While Machine Learning (ML) and Deep Learning (DL) are Artificial Intelligence, the reverse is not true; knowledge graphs or rule engines are artificial bits of intelligence but do not fall under ML or DL, and Deep Learning is a branch of Machine Learning.

AI has evolved many thanks, particularly to the emergence of Cloud Computing and Big Data, inexpensive.

Autonomous Learning

Machine Learning, or machine learning, can reproduce a behavior thanks to algorithms; they fed which decision to make and create a model, the machine can automate the tasks depending on the situation.

In order for a machine to learn the concept of a cat, an engineer compiles a large number of animal examples and passes it on to an algorithm; previously, the engineer had to establish the identity card of a cat and represent these rules in a computer program; today, it just needs to collect the data, which makes the job easier and faster; this new way of automating is leading to considerable progress.

Today, new technologies are robotizing; recently, Oracle launched a stand-alone database, Autonomous Database, which automates data management through machine learning algorithms.

Its data warehouse solution thus reduces human error, and therefore increases security, while allowing DBAs to focus on higher value-added tasks; thanks to the launch of this autonomous data warehouse and its other strengths, Oracle was named a Leader in Data Management Solutions for Analytics by the

2019 Gartner Magic Quadrant, ahead of Snowflake.

Deep Learning

Deep Learning is deep learning; he will seek to understand concepts with more precision by analyzing the data at a high level of abstraction through non-linear understanding.

Its functioning is similar to that of the brain in a neural network; successive layers of data are combined with learning concepts.

The simplest networks have only two layers: an input and an output, knowing that each one can have several hundred, thousands, even millions of neurons; the more they increase, the more the network's capacity to learn more and more abstract representations develop.

To illustrate how deep learning works, imagine that neural networks want to learn to recognize human faces; a first layer sees that there are pixels, the following ones catch several pixels forming an edge, and so on until they acquire the notion of "face"; eventually, they will even be able to distinguish specific faces.

Refer to Machine Learning, and Deep Learning refers to the ability of a machine to learn concepts on its own; this skill is a real technological revolution that is developing, particularly in the areas of Business Intelligence and log file analysis.

Oracle has developed a complete IT Operations Management & Analytics platform integrating numerous Machine Learning algorithms: anomaly detection, synthetic analysis, classification, prediction and correlation.

The notion of deep learning is, first of all, a direct translation of the English term "deep learning," which some people prefer to translate by the notion of statistical learning; like its translation, its definition also varies, but mainly in detail.

Deep learning is a high-level abstraction algorithm that models data from large sets of learned data.

Abstraction assumes that the initial data differs widely from the output data, with the possible image classification, behavior prediction, or translation; abstraction means no simple relationship between input and output.

Modeling means creating a certain realistic scenario so that a realistic classification or result follows; the notion of large learned data sets as input data is extremely diverse. Deep learning or machine learning usually involves important properties of this data being detected during the learning process.

Many terms in this document come from neurological sciences, particularly from the notion of the brain software or virtual machine made up of thousands of units that perform calculations; more specifically, logical and decision-making units link input and output data together through a complex network capable of making complex decisions.

Originally, these systems were called Artificial Neural Networks (ANNs) in order to differentiate them from biological systems, and they generally consist of output data, a narrow network of neurons, and several intermediate layers; these intermediate layers make it possible to deal with complex problems; without them, the system only solves simple calculations.

The number of layers is, therefore, a decisive factor for the complexity of the system and the learning; data binds from layer to layer, the results of one layer serving as input to the next, and so on to lead to complex decision making, this layered operation gives all its depth to the network and the learning process; the adjective "deep" is used herein every sense of the word.

The example above shows three input units, one output, and two middle layers; you see that neurons are "strongly interconnected," which is an essential property of neural networks, this is what allows relationships, functions, or decisions to be complex; without this property, the input-output relationships would be relatively simple.

The goal is not to create an exact model of the brain but to reproduce its ability to learn and recognize complex connections, and a human being can have up to 100 billion neurons that operate at a frequency of around 1 kHz; a modern processor works with 2 billion transistors at 3 GHz.

Note that several prerequisites must be met before a neural network accesses the desired solution; it does not just boil down to "learn and eventually you will find the correct solution," among t is the spiral classification for which the prerequisites are extremely important.

Artificial neuron

The idea of an artificial neuron has not yet been fully specified, and within a processor, the logical unit is made up of transistors; you could also find a "hard-wired" neural network there, but it would have to be "adaptive," it would have to have a "learning capacity."

Indeed, the response of a neuron to incoming impulses must evolve throughout the learning process; this is called "weighting": a neuron evaluates various input variables to obtain the desired output variable; this is why neurons are generally mathematical functions that interconnect input and output variables.

In the learning phase, neurons modify their weighting behavior and refine the output results according to the input variables, and there must therefore be feedback from the overall result that influences each neuron.

We can therefore say that the input and output variables of a neural network are known, but that the values of the neurons, especially in the hidden layers, remain unknown. We are dealing with a "black box."

Taken in isolation, an untrained neural network "knows" nothing and provides random, even chaotic results for the user; only a trained system will provide the desired result if the problem posed is simple, a simple program, easier to debug, will be able to solve it.

A neural network will be used for a more complex problem, trained using large data sets. Each neuron can provide complex output variables and react linearly or non-linearly to the input variables.

This is quite a subtle point, as neurons must be able to react to all possibilities in order to provide a satisfactory result; this implies two things: either the programmer of the neural network knows all the possible connections internal to the network, or he designs the network in a way so complex that it covers "all" the possibilities.

Large datasets

Neural networks are normally used to deal with problems that have some variability, like a human being reacting to a real image; humans have learned to identify certain parts of an image from their experience, that is, from their exposure to a large amount of similar data, with feedback as to how well they are.

Google has access to a huge stock of data as well as immense computing power; at the end of 2016, Google announced that it had tested machine learning techniques for its translation engine; he then found that neural networks trained with relatively small amounts of data provided translation results similar to those of translations based on lexical search and syntax rules.

Through further testing and unsupervised learning, translation errors were reduced by 55-85%. Google has also made its internal TensorFlow software development kit available to the public as open-source software.

Some shortcuts are possible by generating synthetic data from real training data or defining a starting point, such as the number of features neurons should pay attention to or the number of hidden layers in the network.

Artificial Intelligence

Instead, partial aspects are isolated from coping with specific, precise tasks; this is commonly referred to as weak Artificial Intelligence (weak AI).

Neural network

A branch of artificial intelligence research, neuro-informatics, also attempts to further design computers based on the brain model; she sees nervous systems as abstract, freed from their biological properties, and confined to their modes of operation. Artificial neural networks are mainly abstract mathematical methods, a network of neurons.

The biological visual cortex; Deep Learning is a set of techniques that allow a neural network to learn through many layers to identify characteristics.

There are many layers hidden between the entrance and exit of the network, and each is made up of artificial neurons; each layer processes the data, and the results are transmitted to the next one.

The more thicknesses a neural network includes, the more calculations it takes to train it on a CPU; GPUs, TPUs, and FPGAs are also used as hardware accelerators.

Big data

Analyses, in many cases, the flow of information is created from user data collected by companies like Google, Amazon, or Facebook to tailor the offer more precisely to customers.

Traditional computer systems can satisfactorily evaluate such volumes of data: this is why there is a need now for machine learning systems that allow the discovery and realization of previously unknown interrelationships.

Data-Mining

The relevant characteristics must be extracted and evaluated. Data mining differs from machine learning in that it is primarily concerned with applying recognized models while the latter searches for new models.

Different machine learning methods

Developers distinguish between supervised and unsupervised learning with progressive intermediate stages; the algorithms used are very different; supervised learning brings examples, such as a database, to the system.

Developers specify the value of the information, anonymous data; the goal is to reduce the error rate further.

The software obtains better results to the inbox or whether it is placed in the spam folder; such a filtering program is based on Bayesian filters, which is why we speak of Bayesian spam filtering.

Unsupervised learning, that is, unsupervised learning, eliminates the teacher, who in supervised learning always indicates what belongs and gives feedback on the autonomous decisions of the system.

Instead, the program here tries to recognize the patterns on its own, it can use clustering, an item is selected from the amount of data, examined for its characteristics and then compared to those already examined; if it has already examined comparable items, the current object will be added to it; if not, then it is stored separately.

Since a cyber-attack cannot be attributed to a known group, the program can then detect the threat and notify a problem, alarming the user.

Deep learning is more difficult to understand

It is very complex information because it is natural information, such as that which occurs during speech, writing, or facial recognition, biological trained neural networks can be described as deep learning, network is organized into several hierarchical levels; the first level begins with a layer of input.

In the end, more and more refined information reaches the initial level, and the network delivers inlet, and the outlet a, the search of Google in input neurons process the data.

As it cycles through the layers, the filter selects only the information necessary until it can decide end which objects are visible in the image; during the training phase, the developers provide then developers can adapt individual neurons; like our brains, they have different weights and thresholds that can be adjusted in a machine learning system.

ML and

Currently, mainly large companies use these technologies internally, particularly Google; machine learning systems are still too new to be bought as out-of-the-box solutions.

The big Internet service providers are developing their systems and are therefore driving forces in this area; however, despite the commercial interest, some are opting for an open-source approach and working together with independent scientists, advancements play an important role in the choice of specific advertising measures, the greater the amount of data, the more rules and conclusions can generally be drawn from it.

Intelligent programs are needed to deal with such a large number of characteristics, this is where machine learning systems come in: intelligent computer programs recognize trends and can thus give predictions, which can be skewed if they are people.

Indeed, an analyst usually approaches the mass of data with a certain expectation, and these preconceptions are difficult for humans to avoid and often lead to distortions in results; the more data that analysts process, the greater the gap is likely to be.

Even though intelligent machines can also have biases because the latter were formed involuntarily by humans, but with hard facts, they proceed more objectively so that people can fully understand the results of the machine.

In the flood of data, it sometimes becomes difficult to display and organize the results; thus, it can also influence content creation: dynamic systems based on machine learning can create individual experiences.

Website content displayed to the user is still created by editors and designers, but the system integrates components specifically for the user; machine learning systems are also used for self-design:

with the Dreamcatcher project, it is possible to have components designed as part of the customer support through a chatbot.

But in many cases, users are quickly annoyed by operator machines: current chatbot recognition (NLP) can make customers feel like t based on the data collected, machine learning systems may recommend other products to the user; what was previously only possible on a large scale.

So, machine learning has huge better conclusions about the success or failure of campaigns and decisions.

Speed: Analysis takes time if you have to do it manually; machine learning systems increase work speed and allow you to react to changes more quickly.

Automation: Machine learning facilitates operations automation, as modern systems can autonomously adapt to new conditions using machine learning, complex automation processes are also possible.

Individuality: Computer programs can serve countless clients; machine learning those customers; individual recommendations, and specific customer journeys allow better use and optimization of marketing.

Other areas of application of machine learning systems

Thus, machine learning is also increasingly used in marketing, but machine learning they help science and technology drive to simplify our daily lives; the fields of application presented her life shortly.

Science is more important in the natural sciences; the smart processing of big data is a huge machine learning system to record and process more measurement data and detects deviations.

Machine learning also helps in medicine: today, some doctors use artificial intelligence to diagnose and treat patients; machine learning is used to predict diabetes or heart attacks.

Robotics

Robots are now ubiquitous, especially in factories; they help, for example, in mass production to automate consistent work steps; however, they often do not have much to do with smart systems, are only programmed for the precise work step they are performing.

If machine learning systems are used in robotics, these machines must also master new tasks; of course, these developments are also very interesting for other fields: a wide variety of fields.

Traffic

One of the flagship machine learning products is the autonomous car. Vehicles can maneuver independently, and accident-free in real traffic can only be achieved through machine learning; it is impossible to program all situations.

For this reason, it is imperative that cars are meant to back on smart machines, intelligent algorithms, efficient traffic management systems, for example, through intelligent traffic light circuits.

Internet

ML is already playing a major role on the Internet, and spam filters have already been mentioned: through constant learning, spam filters perform better and remove spam more reliably from the inbox.

The same goes for smart virus and malware defense which better protects computers against malware; search engine ranking algorithms, particularly Google's RankBrain, are also machine learning systems; even if the algorithm does not know what to do with the user's, it can guess what might be right for the query.

Personal assistants

Even in our daily lives at home, machine learning computer systems are playing an increasingly important role, how to transform simple apartments into smart homes, Moley Robotics which develops a smart kitchen and prepares meals, also personal assistants such as Google Home and Amazon Echo, with which certain parts of the house can be controlled, use machine learning technologies to understand their users in the best possible way; but many people now ask questions to their smartphones.

Games

Since the beginning of research on artificial intelligence, consoles' ability, game software has been a great motivation for scientists; in chess, checkers, or Chinese Go, machine learning systems were pitted against human opponents.

Computer game developers are also using machine learning to make their games more interesting and the behaviors of human gamers.

Most relevant types of algorithms in business

For some, the following statement seems obvious: one algorithm does not answer all the problems, depending on the type of data and the objectives of your organization, certain models will be more suitable, a linear regression algorithm is easier to train and deploy than others, but it may not be the best for making complex predictions.

The nine machine learning algorithms presented below are among the most used by companies to train their models; these support multiple goals and depend on different learning methods: supervised, unsupervised, semi-supervised, or by reinforcement; these techniques can be combined if necessary.

Supervised learning algorithms

For so-called "supervised" learning, you need known data that already contains the logic you want to apply to a new data set.

Training and testing data set is selected from this data; the first is for setting the algorithm parameters accordingly, while the second is for evaluating the performance of the algorithm; you can also calculate quality metrics there and end the training process if the results are found to be good enough.

The algorithm learns the logic; an algorithm thus trained can then classify the data that has some similarity to the training set with the logic learned, according to the predefined categories Product purchased / not purchased or Cancellation / No cancellation.

Certain steps need to be taken very carefully; when the algorithm is practiced with a training set, it should not just learn everything by heart, but should understand the logic behind it; if you cannot, the problem you face is called over-arming.

Supervised learning models require much groundwork for data scientists; the input datasets must be labeled, the output parameters must be indicated, the expected results; precision must also be adjusted during the learning process.

Some of the simpler tasks are supervised learning, and these tasks can only be performed if the computer receives the correct input-output pairs.

Supervised learning uses labeled images, from which the algorithm must generate a function that delivers the desired result.

However, this method does not allow you to say which input variables should be used to program the algorithm; thus, before the actual "learning," An iterative approach to learning is necessary in order to get an idea of the "relevance" of the results.

A distinction is made between classification algorithms and regression algorithms; as you may have guessed, this type of machine learning requires humans to supervise or train the computer.

Suppose you are working on the design of an autonomous car, you would like the car to be able to distinguish between the different types of road signs.

The intended outcome of the defined exit could be for the car to know the difference between a stop sign and other types of traffic signs, the goal of the machine learning system would be to create an algorithm to accomplish this task; an algorithm is a series of steps required to solve a problem.

To help the computer design the algorithm, humans must teach the computer what a stop sign looks like; the computer first receives images of stop signs and other road signs. Each image is given a label, either "stop" or "non-stop."

In computer parlance, every image is input, the name of the label, "stop" or "non-stop," is what we want the computer to recognize later, for stop signs.

Once an algorithm has been created, artificial intelligence engineers put it to the test with new data, and the algorithm should be able to identify images of stop signs that it has never seen before; if he is not able to do this, he needs additional training, and does that remind you of something?

You might be wondering if machine learning is effective at accomplishing this task; the percentage of correct solutions is called accuracy. For example, if machine learning recognizes 98 out of 100 stop signs, the accuracy is 98%.

When humans use images to train a computer to see, we are talking about computer vision, and computer vision does not just make it possible to build self-driving cars; it also helps computers read handwriting.

Supervised machine learning can also be used for forecasting, and a company could use machine learning to forecast the number of years its employees will remain in its service.

Machine learning could then analyze different criteria, such as education and years of experience, the algorithm that will be created by machine learning can be used when hiring new employees.

The biggest disadvantage of supervised machine learning is that it must have data labeled correctly for the system to train; a data labeling study found that people spent up to 80% of their time making sure the labels were accurate.

Linear regression

Without a doubt, linear regression algorithms are the most used by data science teams; they make simple correlations between two variables in a dataset; a set of inputs and the corresponding outputs are examined and quantified to show a relationship, such as changing one variable affects another.

Its simplicity explains the popularity of linear regression. The algorithm is easily explained, relatively transparent, and has few parameters to configure; well known in statistics, this algorithm is often used to forecast sales or risks.

Support Vector Machine (SVM)

Support Vector Machines or SVMs (Wide Margin Separators) are algorithms that separate data into classes; during training, an

SVM finds a line that separates a set's data into specific classes and maximizes the margins of each class; after learning the classification lines, the model can then apply them to the new data.

Experts place SVM in the category of "linear classifiers": the algorithm is ideal for identifying simple classes that it separates by vectors called hyperplanes.

It is also possible to program the algorithm for nonlinear data, which vectors cannot separate; but, with hypercomplex training data - faces, personality traits, genomes, and genetic material - class systems are getting smaller and harder to identify and require a little more human assistance.

Support vector machines are widely used in finance, and they offer great precision on current and future data; the associated models can be used to virtually compare relative financial performance, value, and return on investment, so-called nonlinear SVMs are often used to classify images or words, sentences, and entities .

Decision tree

A decision tree algorithm graphs the data in branches to show the possible outcomes of various actions; it classifies and predicts response variables based on past decisions.

This visual method has proven itself, the results of the decision trees are easy to explain; citizen data scientists will have no trouble interpreting them; decisions and their likely impacts on a result are readily visible, even when the input datasets turn out to be incomplete.

However, decision trees become difficult to read when associated with large volumes of data and complex variables; this is why they are used for low-stakes decisions, such as anticipating changes in loan rates or market reactions if a company changes an important part of its products.

Unsupervised learning algorithms

Algorithms that use unsupervised learning can structure a customer database based on different customer groups; algorithms themselves decide the number of clusters.

Another possibility for unsupervised learning is so-called dimensional reduction, and this can be used to find what are called characteristics from an existing data set, that is, items in which the data differs, an example of this could be the description of clothing, then the color would be extracted as a characteristic.

Unsupervised machine learning is used to find trends in data that are difficult to label; human language is a type of data, each person has their particular language, this is why it is difficult to tell a computer exactly how a word should be pronounced.

There is no previously known or labeled data here; this is the usual meaning of "deep learning," the algorithm is in a way self-taught, and the tools somehow attempt to find classifications within data without any prior knowledge.

A marketing algorithm could use unsupervised learning to identify segments of prospects with similar buying habits.

The machine goes through the data without any clues and tries to discover recurring patterns or trends; this approach is commonly used in some areas, such as cybersecurity.

Among the unsupervised models, we distinguish the algorithms of clustering, association, and dimensional reduction.

Medicine is another example; when looking for a cure or the origin of a particular disease, scientists try to determine whether that disease involves specific genes.

Genes contain the information that makes you the person you are, each of your cells contains 25,000 to 35,000 genes, researchers can use unsupervised machine learning to look for similarities in the genes of people with this disease.

Or in other words, the output is undefined; the system takes the raw data and then looks for patterns on its own; once it detects a pattern, an algorithm is developed, and the algorithm can then be used in a manner comparable to supervised machine learning.

The data scientist does not train so-called unsupervised algorithms; they depend on deep learning methods to identify patterns by combing through unlabeled training data sets and then observing the correlations; models trained with this method are not directed to find a particular result or identify particular data.

This data mining algorithm looks for affinities between two dataset elements to identify a negative or positive correlation.

The algorithm is widely used by sales teams looking to know which products one customer will possibly acquire with another; if a high percentage of customers who buy bread also buy butter, then the algorithm can conclude that the purchase of product A will often be followed by that of product B , this data can be crossed into data sets, data points and buying ratios.

Such an algorithm can also determine that the acquisition of item A has a 10% exchange rate driving the purchase of a product C; marketing teams can use this information to develop layout strategies of products in a store.

The distribution in K-means (K-means)

The K-means algorithm uses an iterative method to sort data points into groups based on similar characteristics, and such a model would classify the web results of the word talisman into one group relating to an object with protective virtues and another to the car model produced by the Renault group, the Renault Talisman sedan.

The K-means breakdown has a reputation for being precise while being able to handle groups of data in a relatively short period, this type of algorithm is used equally well by search engine publishers to provide relevant results or by companies that want to classify user behavior; this technique is also effective in the context of IT performance analysis.

Semi-supervised learning algorithms

Semi-supervised learning methods combine labeled and unlabeled data, algorithms of this type feed on certain information thanks to labeled categories, suggestions, and examples; then, they create their labels by exploring the data on their own, following a rudimentary diagram or the indications of data scientists.

Generative antagonistic networks

Generative adversarial networks are models that mimic the distribution of data; two networks are placed in competition to determine the best solution to a problem; one of the neural networks called a generator feeds on the input data to generate a good output, while the second, the discriminator, relies on the output of the first to find faults and improve it.

An engineer specifies the dimensions and parameters to fabricate the structure of a part, which he will then print in three dimensions; this process allows you to iterate until you find the shape, structure, or even the ideal materials to put it into production; in audiovisual production, this technique makes it possible to generate faces, objects or pieces of music.

Naive Bayesian Classifier

The naive Bayesian classifier is based on Bayes' theorem based on conditional probability, and researchers use this algorithm to recognize classes of objects on labeled datasets; then the algorithm is trained on unlabeled data; once this cycle is complete, the researchers match the tags and restart the workout; this technique is particularly used in the context of natural language processing or to label datasets without using services such as Amazon Mechanical Turk.

Reinforcement learning

A less important type of learning in economics and is also a controlled procedure; the idea here is to reward successful behaviors while suppressing those that lead to undesirable results.

To play for real money on ten one-armed bandits, you would first play them five times on each machine, then more often on the machines that produced the highest gains in the first repetition; the algorithm can also play a bit on machines that produced little or no payoff, as it could have been an unfortunate coincidence in the first five attempts, and in reality, these are the best machines.

Reinforcement learning algorithms are based on reward and punishment systems, the algorithm is assigned a goal and seeks to move closer to it for maximum reward.

He relies on limited information and learns from his previous actions, these algorithms can depend on a scheme (a model); they must then follow predefined steps, and the number of errors and trials is limited, others do not rely on a diagram and interpret with each new try.

The third type of ML is reinforcement machine learning; in this type of machine learning, self-supervised learning systems can improve without human supervision.

In this case, the algorithm learns by repeatedly trying to achieve a specific goal, and as he tries to get as many rewards as possible, he gradually improves.

Again, this task may seem easy to you. But a robot must be able to consider many things to perform this task; it must first be able to locate and pick up an object and consider its grip strength, the strength of the throw, and the weight and shape of the object.

All of this requires understanding several principles of physics, it would be difficult to create a program capable of taking all these criteria into account; this is why this task is well suited for self-directed machine learning.

Robots using self-supervised machine learning would be useful in places like sorting centers, where they could sort materials.

Another well-known example is when a computer beats a human at a game; Computers can use self-directed machine learning to find the easiest way to win a game; two computers can even play one against each other using self-supervised machine learning.

Self-directed machine learning is used in many areas to improve systems, one of these areas is computer security, also known as cybersecurity.

It is very important to keep confidential data safe, especially data used by banks and government; self-guided machine learning can pretend to be a hacker and thus show humans the flaws in the system before a real hacker finds them.

So how could self-directed machine learning be used in our self-driving car example?

He could create virtual driving simulations to check if the autonomous car stops when his camera sees a red octagonal sign.

Q-Learning

Q-Learning algorithms seek to find the best method to achieve a defined objective while seeking to obtain maximum rewards; they attempt as many actions as possible per system state without having any initial knowledge of the environment; an algorithm like this can be built to get rewards quickly or to achieve a major goal.

Q-Learning is often associated with Deep Learning models as part of research projects, including those of Google DeepMind; this technique is then available in various algorithms, including "deep deterministic policy gradient or hindsight experience replay.

Model-based algorithm

Unlike Q-Learning, model-based algorithms have limited freedom to create states and actions, and this nevertheless gives them greater statistical efficiency; they are trained with specific data and basic actions from the environment through supervised training; in principle, this speeds up learning, such an algorithm can serve as a benchmark for the deployment of a digital twin.

Algorithm

Some problems can easily be formulated into an algorithm, such as it is very difficult to recognize a font or a keyword; here, machine learning procedures help, algorithms have long been developed that analyze existing data and apply the resulting knowledge to new data.

Learning algorithms

A machine learning algorithm has a lot of freedom, so-called parameters, in a simplified manner; typically, machine learning algorithms use several hundred, there are many different learning methods; only vector machines and supporting decision trees, as representatives of supervised learning, need to be mentioned here.

There are different algorithms for each of these methods to adjust the parameters to get the best possible agreement; these algorithms are the actual learning procedures in machine learning.

Depending on the purpose of the application, some algorithms are more or less efficient, the data can also influence it; some special applications even require modifications themselves.

Manual labor

As automated as it sounds, machine learning processes still involve many manual steps, and; this is why data usually needs to be cleaned up first, as part of data cleansing.

Statistical method

Many repetitions lead to good results, and computers can do this dumb job very well, with the greatly increased computational capacity, we do not have to wait very long for results.

While management defines machine learning as part of company strategy, machine learning - combined with the right data - has the power to revolutionize the entire business model.

With all the possibilities that should not be forgotten: ML is not a panacea, the decisive factor is the quality of the data, that is, the fodder of the ML: thus, garbage in - garbage out applies particularly to the ML; in addition, money laundering requires very large amounts of data,

It is critical to find the right use case for the business and then design iteratively, using whatever knowledge exists in the field.

ML Main stages

Data preparation

Data Collection: First, gather the data you will need for machine learning; make sure you put them together in a consolidated form, so they are all contained in one Flat Table.

Reconciliation: This is about preparing data to make it usable by machine learning algorithms.

Data cleaning: find Nulls, missing values , duplicate data, replace Nulls and missing values with other values, and make sure there are no duplicates.

Data decomposition: columns of text sometimes contain more than one piece of information; we must therefore divide them into as many dedicated columns as necessary; if some columns represent categories, convert them to category type columns.

Data aggregation: group certain information together when relevant.

Data Scaling: This will provide data at a common scale; it is necessary when a great variation in the features ranges.

Formatting and transformation: from categorical to digital.

Data Enrichment: Sometimes, you will need to enrich existing data with external data to give the algorithm more information, which improves the model.

Feature Engineering

View your data as a whole to see if there are any links between the columns; by using charts, you can see the characteristics/features side by side and detect any link between the features and between the features and the labels.

The links between a feature and the label allow us to see if a feature will strongly affect the result; sometimes, you will need to generate additional features from those that already exist in a classification.

But if you have thousands of columns, you will need to apply a dimension reduction; there are several techniques for doing this, including Principal Component Analysis (PCA); PCR is an unsupervised learning algorithm that uses existing columns to generate new columns, called principal components, which can be used later by the classification algorithm.

Algorithm choice

Divide your dataset into three parts: training, testing, and validation.

The validation data will only be used at the very end of the process and will, unless necessary, very rarely be examined and used beforehand in order to avoid introducing any bias into the result.

Choose the relevant algorithm (s).

Try out the algorithms with different combinations of parameters and compare the performance of their results.

Use the hyperparameter procedure to try out many combinations, and find the one that works best, as soon as you are reasonably satisfied with a model, save it even if it is not perfect, as you may never find the combination that got you there again.

Continue testing after each new model, and if the results are not satisfactory, you can start over: at the hyperparameter stage if you are lucky.

It is also possible to have to start over from the choice of features to include or even review the state of our data.

When embarking on a machine learning process, it is important to keep in mind that our data may not allow us to achieve a better result than what we are already getting with our classic methods already in place, but it certainly does reveal some interesting insights to us during the data analysis process.

ML Techniques

Machine learning is the latest advancement in computing that uses state-of-the-art methodologies to improve business performance; as machine learning algorithms are relatively new.

These techniques are constantly iterated to improve the user experience; continuous updates and developments not only overwhelm newbies but make it difficult for experts to keep abreast of new advancements.

Based on mathematical expressions, the machine learning algorithm provides data-centric insights into a problem or obstacle; consider the following example, which perfectly demonstrates the use and application of the machine learning algorithm.

Regression

I help predict the future from current data, and it also helps you find the correlation between two variables to define the cause and effect relationship; you can plot a graph based on these variables and continuously forecast based on the predictor variable.

However, there are different forms of regression, ranging from linear regression and complex regression, including calculating and representing polynomial data; you should always start with the basics, which is mastering linear regression, and then move on to complex shapes.

Common examples of linear regression are:

Weather forecast

Forecast market trends

Identify potential risks

Classification

The method sets a class value based on the input data, and it will give you definitive predictions about a certain stock; it will tell you whether the visitor will become a customer or not.

However, the classification is not based on just two categories but multiples due to its probability calculation, it can help you determine if the given image contains a flower or a leaf; the classification method will give you three likely results: 1) flower, 2) leaf, 3) none.

Grouping

K-Means is the most popular method of grouping input data, which allows you to fix the value of K and order the data according to that value.

Dimensionality reduction

The more complex the results will be which will make it difficult to consolidate them; the selection and extraction of features are at the heart of dimensionality reduction in machine learning, and they allow the elimination of irrelevant variables; if you need to predict the risk of weight gain in a group of people.

It uses a large number of variables such as email titles, content, and template, among others; but the algorithm may overlap with some factors that can affect the result; so, to reduce the chances of repetition and provide you with accurate results.

Overall method

It is a technique of stacking data using predictor variables from various models; it, therefore, combines various predictive models to form a very precise and optimized predictive output; the method is used to make decisions taking into account various factors.

You are considering buying a property in town, and the ensemble method will predict your response based on various factors such as type of property, value, savings, long term investment goals, and economic conditions; the method is used to find the most precise answer to a problem in different scenarios, so you can change the value of each variable each time to predict the results or responses.

The Random Forest algorithm is a typical example of ensemble methods that combine various decision trees based on multiple data sets; as a result, the predictive output is much better than the estimates from a single decision tree.

A single machine learning algorithm may be accurate in one situation, but the result may be grossly incorrect in another context, so, to minimize such inaccuracies, scientists are using the set method for more corrective prediction: Kaggle, an online ML competition portal, incorporated the set method to score participants.

Neural networks and deep learning

Unlike linear models, the neural network is based on a complex, divisional data model; it includes multiple layers of a parameter to provide you with unique and precise output; however, the model is still based on linear regression but uses multiple hidden layers; that is why it has called a neural network.

The term deep learning indicates the complex knowledge required to summarize these multiple parameters.

Deep learning scientists need high-level graphics processing units to process large amounts of data; this is why these techniques are very successful in genres related to images, sound, and video.

ML uses

You probably do not even notice machine learning going on in your everyday life, that spam filter in your inbox is machine learning; machine learning is also already present in the United States alone, there are 47.3 million adults who have access to a smart speaker; however, ML is having a big impact on some industries in our world.

Financial

Machine learning can very easily streamline internal processes within the financial industry due to the large amount of data that the industry collects; banks and financial institutions use machine learning to detect fraud through data mining; a recent report indicated that within the next 15 years, robots would be able to perform 75% of jobs in financial services through machine learning.

Government

A recent Deloitte article states, "Governments collect vast amounts of data on everything from health care, housing and education to national and homeland security, both directly and through organizations to nonprofit.

Health

Wearable devices and sensors are making machine learning a growing trend in healthcare; these devices help healthcare professionals identify trends that can help diagnose a patient, resulting in better treatment options.

With large databases of images in radiology, machine learning can quickly assess images that would take longer for medical experts to process.

Through machine learning, Google trained computers to detect cancer in patients with 89% accuracy, Stanford uses a method of deep learning an algorithm to predict skin cancer and when patients will die to improve palliative care.

Transport

ML analyzes the driver's GPS, where the package is delivered when the customer receives the package, its speed, and the weather to find the most efficient route possible for the delivery person.

ML Criticisms

With all of machine learning's outstanding achievements, the app has to come under criticism; machine learning is creating a crisis in science, a growing body of scientific research is using machine learning on data that has already been collected; the solutions proposed by these scientists are wrong because they are only applicable in this dataset, not in the real world.

ML future

It becomes evident that there are also ethical responsibilities that we must take on.

What will happen if this technology becomes a monopoly?

Will this technology be accessible only to those who are wealthy?

What if the machine learning critics are right and another AI winter comes true?

Each process or technique has advantages and disadvantages, even in the case of machine learning; certain factors lead to advantages or disadvantages.

Identifying trends and patterns

ML makes it possible to manage a large amount of data and to understand trends and patterns that would not have been possible to handle this large amount of data by humans.

In the e-commerce industry, it helps to understand and manage its marketing activities according to the user's needs; like offers, products, several clicks, offers, coupons and based on all these options, the growth of the business is ultimately dependent.

Due to the machine learning technique, instead, let him make his own decision without our intervention; hence, it helps them develop and improve their decision-making ability on their own and correct mistakes.

Continuous improvement

Composed of a machine learning algorithm, it helps the system to understand errors and correct those errors constantly; therefore, it increases efficiency and precision; if we design a weather forecast app and it gives us regular weather forecasts; the accuracy of this prediction depends entirely on standard error checking and improved accuracy.

The machine learning algorithm helps manage and improve a large amount of multidimensional data and improve their skills to avoid errors using AI technology.

Wide application

ML can be useful for those who are working in the e-commerce field or for healthcare providers, they can use ML to get huge help in growing their market, and it also helps in increasing l efficiency of human labor; using this app gives customers a very personal experience to use it while targeting the right customers.

ML Disadvantages

Some of the drawbacks one is even faced with in the field of the machine learning process, factors that impact BA are:

Data acquisition

In the process of ML, a large amount of data is used in the training and learning process; therefore, the use of data must be of good quality and impartial; during the process of machine learning with the help of software development services, there are also times when we have to wait; during this period, new data is generated and can be used for a different process.

Time and resources

During the machine learning procedure, the algorithms that help manage all functions to manage data and the use of certain data in rectification in case of errors take time and reliable and reliable resources for the operation of this system.

Interpretation

When algorithms help in all of these processes and give result-ant output, this given output should be checked for any errors, and the correcting operation should be followed to achieve the desired accuracy; and when selecting this algorithm, we need to select this algorithm which you need for this purpose.

High sensitivity to errors

In the process of machine learning hence, there is a huge chance to encounter any errors because while you train your dataset to this particular number of algorithms, if there is an error in the algorithm, it can lead the user to multiple irrelevant ads.

These errors are a common problem that occurs repeatedly, when these errors occur, finding the main source for which the problem was created is not easy, and finding that particular problem and fixing it takes longer.

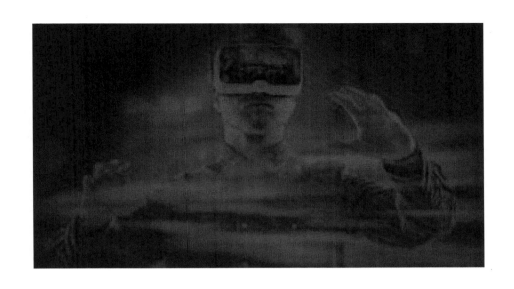

CHPATER 3: VIRTUAL REALITY

Virtual Reality

VR is associated with video games; you adjust your helmet, overcome obstacles, and kill as many enemies as possible; some music videos and 3D movies also rely on VR. However, computer-simulated reality endings are not just for fun.

In the military field, this advanced technology is used, for example, to train airplane pilots and parachutists.

In the health field, she helps surgeons before surgery and helps treat some patients with uncontrollable fear such as agoraphobia, arachnophobia, or acrophobia, and commercial applications are also increasing.

Some transportation companies and insurance companies use virtual reality for advertising purposes to catapult the customer inside their vehicles or to educate them about real dangers like traffic accidents; VR also has its place in education, especially in the context of virtual videoconferences, and in architecture to visit buildings before their construction.

Virtual reality is a technology that uses software to create a virtual environment, and it creates some artificial senses such as touch, hearing, and sight; the world of virtual reality merges the power of 3D graphics.

Virtual reality technology is widely used for different purposes, such as games, engineering, entertainment, education, design, movies, media, and medicine, and more; Virtual reality has made various important changes in the lives of humans and their daily activities, there are mainly three types of VR systems: VR Video Mapping, Immersive VR, and Desktop VR.

How does virtual reality work?

The virtual reality headset has the difficult task of sending you into a virtual environment by making you believe that the scenes there are real; how does this accessory exercise its power of persuasion?

Your eyes see the same images, but not quite at the same angle to achieve depth, and parallax also contributes to depth; this technique consists of setting certain objects in motion more slowly to accentuate the distance that separates them from the user.

The realism of the movements is obtained with several sensors: the gyroscope for the angles, the accelerometer for 3D movements, and the magnetometer to detect the position of the helmet; these sensors are grouped under the name head-tracking; on the audio side, immersion is ensured by specialized sound which reproduces noises from different angles depending on the user's position.

Virtual reality is sometimes called VR, computer-simulated reality, or immersive multimedia, and it is sometimes wrongly confused with augmented reality, which is based on a real environment with the addition of virtual elements.

Virtual reality is a technology that allows a person to be immersed in an artificial world created digitally, and it is not augmented reality.

It can be a copy of the real world or an imaginary universe; the experience is visual and auditory, and, in some cases, haptic with the production of effects feedback, when the person is equipped with the appropriate interfaces, they experience certain sensations related to touch or certain actions.

Virtual reality is a technology that uses software to create a virtual environment, and it creates some artificial senses such as touch, hearing, and sight, the world of virtual reality merges the power of 3D graphics.

Virtual reality technology is widely used for different purposes, such as games, engineering, entertainment, education, design, movies, media, medicine and more.

Virtual reality has made various important changes in the lives of humans and their daily activities; there are mainly three types of VR systems: VR Video Mapping, Immersive VR, and Desktop VR.

Virtual reality headsets

This immersion is done through a virtual reality headset which places a 3D display system on the nose, in front of the eyes; some models are equipped with sensors that detect movement to allow the user to look around.

Virtual reality rooms

There are also virtual reality rooms in which the images are projected on the walls, the floor, and the ceiling with a motion capture system used to adjust the perspective according to the movements.

Virtual reality and its applications: video games, simulators, Etc.

Virtual reality for the general public has boomed since 2015 with the arrival of headsets that are both more efficient and affordable, and Google has played the democratization card by offering a cardboard model called Cardboard which is used with a smartphone as a display system.

Several manufacturers, including Samsung (Gear VR), HTC (HTC Vive), Sony (PlayStation VR), and Oculus (Oculus Rift), have released headsets equipped with motion sensors mainly intended for video games and recreational applications, more expensive, they are connected to a computer or a game console.

Virtual reality also has many other applications: training with simulators, treatment of phobias, simulation of surgical procedures, architecture, archeology with the reconstruction of sites, virtual visits to museums, Etc.

The term virtual reality encompasses a series of computer technologies that aim to immerse one or more people in a virtual environment created by software, an environment that more or less faithfully reproduces a real setting.

The user accesses the virtual setting through a virtual reality headset; for total immersion, virtual reality does not only use the view of the environment recreated by software.

VR Pros and Cons

Advantages

Better than reality

The visuals seen there are much better than the reality Virtual reality technology is used in video games, and the user feels they are in another world, in video games by virtual reality game controller, the transmission of vibrations and other sensations provide the user with a great gaming experience; you can also have real gaming experiences such as user fighting against zombies.

Used in different fields

Virtual reality has been used in different fields due to its extensive functionality; it is also used in the military, education, and various other fields; it adds more dimensions to different areas; virtual reality is used in aviation and architecture to visualize the end product.

The user has incredible experiences.

Users have huge experiences in using virtual reality; users feel like they are experiencing real places, hearing real sounds, and seeing real things; many feel that they are using virtual reality technology more and more.

People highly regard her with disabilities because by using virtual reality, they can explore the real world; films produced for VR allow the audience to see everything around them in every scene; thus, it creates an interactive visualization experience for the audience.

Provided detailed views

Virtual reality offers a complete and detailed view of the place, virtual reality makes tourist sites easier and more interesting, it offers a detailed description of the place you want to visit; users can then plan their trip by seeing the actual locations for that location; additionally, users can see important landmarks and places they are interested in going.

Connect to people

Virtual reality gives chances to communicate with people you do not know in real life; it helps form new relationships more effectively than real life; users come to know about different types of people and connect with them.

Effective communication

One of the main advantages of Virtual Reality is effective communication; users can communicate with each other and thus enjoy their discussions, which provides a new experience of communicating with people.

Disadvantages

High price

One of the main disadvantages of virtual games is that they are not affordable for everyone, they are expensive, and people who cannot buy them will not access this technology.

Communication should not be replaced for the group of people

Another disadvantage of virtual reality is that communication using this technology should not be replaced; dishonesty is likely there.

Feeling of worthlessness

So many times, VR users feel worthless; they feel that they are escaping the real world, and sometimes this feeling is very dangerous.

Users get hooked on the virtual world.

Users navigate a non-virtual environment; this addiction can cause various health problems.

The technology is still experimental.

Although virtual reality is used in different fields, it is still experimental and not yet accepted or fully developed; VR has many downsides, so it is not yet fully accepted.

Training in a VR environment is not real.

Another disadvantage of VR is that a person who has been trained in a VR environment can do well in that environment but cannot do well in the real world; hence, it does not give the same results in real life compared to a Virtual Reality environment.

VR creation tools

Nowadays, creating virtual experiences is within everyone's reach, long reserved for programming and graphic design specialists; many tools now exist to allow common users to create, more and more easily, virtual worlds rich in interactivity.

Ranging from the simple experience of a 360 ° photo taken with their mobile phone to a complex and realistic simulation of a work environment, teachers have various tools at their disposal to create and integrate virtual learning situations.

In their classes, the following article provides a non-exhaustive list of the most popular virtual experience creation tools; the offer is large, and the platforms are not created equal.

It is, therefore, important to have a point of reference in order to understand the differences and the advantages of each one in order to make an informed choice according to their needs and capacities.

This list is not ordered in any particular way; indeed, since the different platforms available today vary enormously in functionality, level of expertise and concrete application, it would be not easy to rank them from the best to the least effective.

This list is therefore intended to be an overview of the tools most used today; there, you will find comparisons of costs, features, and levels of expertise required.

This article only discusses platforms that allow users to create virtual reality experiences themselves and not those of companies that offer turnkey services; a sorting was also done in order to list mainly the tools used in the educational environment.

Virtual experiences platforms

Unity logo

Unity is one of the most popular platforms for creating virtual and augmented reality experiences; if you play games, you have already tried one of the games made with this platform; on his site, we can see that creations with Unity have been downloaded to more than 3 billion devices and that AR and VR experiences represent 60% of the content created.

To make the process easier, Unity last year developed a new toolkit for building common AR and VR interactions, the popularity of this platform comes mainly from its low cost, students can use it for free at any time, and self-employed people can also use it for free if they earn less than $ 100,000 in income.

Teachers must complete an educational license application to manage student projects and install the platform on more than two devices; additionally, Unity does not charge any royalties following the sale of games created with its platform.

Regarding the level of expertise required, getting started requires some knowledge of programming and 3D modeling; however, Unity's user sharing community is very large, and we can easily find answers to our questions or help with our projects.

Script pages and digital assets are available for free, and countless video tutorials can be found on YouTube; we can choose from 25 different export formats, depending on the devices on which we want to make our creation available; Unity is a downloadable computer application that is mainly used for designing video games, but also for simulations and 3D movies.

Unreal Engine

Unreal Engine is also one of the most popular platforms for creating video games and virtual experiences; similar to Unity, it differs on a few points, especially in graphics quality; indeed, the characters will be more realistic and the textures richer with Unreal Engine than with Unity.

The other divergence concerns the business model, as with Unity, it is possible to create games for free, but Unreal Engine charges 5% royalties on all revenue generated after $ 3,000 of revenue per quarter, including in-app purchases and other sources of revenue in addition to the sale price, however, in education, this is not a disadvantage if the tool is used only for teaching and learning and free sharing of designed educational virtual experiences.

The expertise level required is quite high, and you will need to be proficient in the C ++ programming language; however, one of the advantages of Unreal Engine is the presence of templates in the Blueprint editing interface to create a game without using a single line of code.

Blueprint is a visual programming language that uses boxes and arrows to represent digital entities and the links between them; thus, the boxes already contain the lines of codes that will display the entities on the screen, and the arrows contain the interaction codes between the objects. Another advantage of Unreal Engine is the ability to edit your creation in virtual mode.

You have to use a wired virtual reality headset, such as the Oculus Rift or the HTC Vive, then you can easily launch the editor in your headset and move or edit objects in the virtual space, the sharing community is not as comprehensive as Unity's, but help and tutorials are easy to find, Unreal Engine is a downloadable computer application that is primarily used to create very realistic games and complex virtual experiences such as simulations.

Sumerian

Sumerian is an AR and VR experience creation web platform developed by Amazon; a novice user will create a simple virtual experience within hours, using the visual programming language; creation is easier than with Unity and Unreal Engine, but the rendering is also less realistic.

One of the advantages of Sumerians is the integration of virtual chatbots available in twenty languages; these characters move their body and their lips according to the text to be spoken, so no need to program this interaction yourself.

This feature can be useful in education to add a teacher or a virtual guide to the created experience. Pricing is a bit complicated to calculate, as it depends on the storage space used, the number of visits, and other parameters; the free plan can host up to 50MB of data for up to 100 views per month for one year; nevertheless, according to the calculations presented as an example on the site, the publication costs [22] [23] are not prohibitive.

CoSpaces Edu

CoSpaces Edu is a web platform for creating augmented and virtual reality experiences, developed primarily for everyone; it is now aimed at education only; the advantage of this tool is that it is available on mobile devices for viewing and authoring.

Each change is visible in real-time on each device; in addition, as CoSpaces Edu is designed for education, the teacher can create classes, give exercises that are automatically identified with the student's name, group students into teams on a project, and intervene in real-time in the process.

Since last year, creative space for students, the platform has partnered with MergeVR to create augmented experiences triggered on the Merge Cube; the application is translated into a few languages, especially French.

The business plan is based on an annual subscription depending on the number of seats desired; but it is limited to 30 seats, creating a single class and 2 CoSpaces, and a limited collection of 3D objects.

The tool is very easy to use and is very suitable for all levels of education, even elementary school; CoSpaces Edu has its visual programming language, blocks, which resembles that of Scratch.

It allows actions and interactions to be easily coded using already programmed blocks of code that are dropped one after the other according to the desired task processing logic; expert users can write lines of script themselves to further enhance the platform's interactivity capabilities. CoSpaces Edu is a web platform used in all subjects for creations as diverse as virtual museums, escape games, reconstructions of historical places, mathematical representations, Etc.

Update

Upscale Is a web platform for creating virtual educational experiences, working with a 360 ° or 180 ° video or photo, it is possible to add clickable hotspots that will display, for example, an information text or a multiple-choice question; the studio interface is very intuitive and allows a novice user to quickly learn to use it to create an interactive virtual quiz.

Although you cannot program an object manipulation like with Unity or Unreal Engine, Upscale is an excellent tool for the simplicity of starting a virtual educational experience, and this can be integrated with all eLearning management platforms such as Moodle and be viewable on the web via any device online or offline with the free Upscale Player mobile app.

There are also tools for tracking the use of deployed experiences; we will therefore have a good overview of the effectiveness of the interactions. The studio's education version is accessible by annual subscription at 1000 € for 100 students.

VIAR360

VIAR360 is a web platform for creating virtual experiences similar to Upscale; indeed, creation relies on uploading 360 ° media and adding hotspots; you do not need to know a programming language, but if you do, you will have more editing options; one of the advantages of VIAR360 is the possibility of integrating interactive modules created with H5P.

This free platform allows you to perform quizzes easily, simple games, graphics, timelines, Etc.

Experiences can be viewed on the web, mobile device, or VR headset; they can also be viewed offline with the free mobile app; pricing is based on a US $ 99 monthly subscription that allows three publishers to create an unlimited number of virtual experiences playable up to 50 times.

Tour creator & Google epeditions

Tour Creator is a Google web platform for creating guided virtual tours, very easy to use. Just import 360 ° or 180 ° images and add points of interest to display text or images; you can even use the images from Google Street View.

The tours created can be easily shared with a URL link or exported to Google Expeditions to provide a guided tour for students; this free application allows users connected to the same wireless network to take a virtual tour guided by the teacher.

Story Spheres

Story Spheres is a web platform for creating sound virtual tours, very easy to use; import 360 ° images and add points of interest that will trigger a soundtrack such as narration, description, animal cry, Etc.

Tilt Brush

Tilt Brush is a virtual reality creation app powered by Google. It is available on VR headsets such as Oculus Rift, Oculus Quest, HTC Vive, Windows Mixed Reality, and Valve Index. It unlocks creativity with 6 degrees of freedom.

The user can move around, and within their virtual creation, tilt Brush offers a wide range of brushes with different textures, even some that are dynamic, and pre-built environments, such as a tailoring mannequin and pedestal.

Mainly used in the visual arts, this application is suitable for both novices and experts alike since the interface is intuitive, and by activating the expert features, the most experienced virtual artists will achieve very complex achievements.

Creations can be shared on the web through Google Poly or exported to 3D modeling applications such as Unity for use in a game or other virtual experience or 3D printing.

VR headsets can also record video and images captured on the device; the modalities differ from device to device, but you can easily create animation and use video editing software to add narration; artists from all over the world even perform creative live performances in front of an audience.

Gravity Sketch

Gravity Sketch is a virtual 3D modeling application used via a virtual reality headset such as the Oculus Quest, Oculus Rift, HTC Vive, Windows Mixed Reality, and Varjo; this powerful tool allows you to make and edit 3D models inside of a virtual interface.

Collaborative creation is possible with most devices, and pricing is based either on the one-time purchase of the application, called Core, and with functionalities limited among others to 4 layers and four environments, or a monthly subscription.

This subscription comes in two versions, Pro and Studio, where the latter is the most expensive and the most comprehensive.

For the educational sector, a 6-month trial version is available, and an education rate depending on the number of seats desired will be negotiated subsequently by contacting the company; 3D models can be exported in different formats for use elsewhere such as with Unity or directly to other 3D modeling applications like Sketchfab.

VR legitimacy in medicine

It allows, through a headset, to immerse the user in 360 degrees in moving and sound images, by assisting treatments, improving the training of practitioners, or even bringing a more fun dimension to care, could virtual reality be the dream tool of health professionals and patients?

VR health Applications

Thanks to virtual reality, it is now possible to treat many disorders through immersive therapeutic applications; some clinics, for example, use virtual reality for exposure therapy; it is about confronting the patient with the source of his trauma in a gradual way in order to make him adopt a new behavior.

This cognitive technology is used in functional therapy in the context of loss of motor skills.

The Trois Prime e-health agency works on the reintegration of patients with neurodegenerative, psychiatric, and injury diseases such as stroke and trauma; she has developed VTOPIA Neuro, a platform that offers both solutions applied to the rehabilitation of impaired cognitive functions as well as medical decision support tools in head trauma.

A very concrete example: the patient is immersed in a virtual reality kitchen, which will allow the practitioner to observe him in the situation.

The patient's mission, is to follow a recipe intended to see how he plans his actions; the practitioner will thus be able to identify the difficulties encountered and suggest areas for improvement in real-time to work on the patient's autonomy gradually.

This technology is also applicable to the treatment of phobias, fear of airplanes, of driving, of heights, of spiders.

This technology is very effective in that it can virtually project the patient into a universe where his phobia is translated very realistically.

Imagined with the therapists, the scenarios that the patient will be confronted with will create repetition and an intensity that will gradually allow him to accept the situation that blocked him in reality.

Relieve and treat pain

In October 2017, a Swiss research team succeeded in showing the effectiveness of virtual reality to treat phantom pain occurring in amputees or paraplegics.

Thus, a visual stimulus coupled with a tactile stimulus would give the illusion of feeling its limbs and reduce this pain for which there is no cure, composed of a pair of legs, a camera, and a headset, their device relies on the illusion.

Flmed by the camera in real-time, the legs appear to the patient's eyes as his own; at the same time, the scientist simultaneously taps the patient's back and the dummy legs: the illusion is created after a minute, and the pain subsides.

Medical training for healthcare professionals

Thanks to virtual reality, medical schools have applications for their students and interns; the objective, for example: to offer medical intern specific emergencies in order to assess his emergency diagnosis, his decision-making, and the actions performed; through these programs, students can safely face situations where their composure is assessed.

In addition, many virtual reality simulations are dedicated to learning medicine, whether it is training in surgery through the simulation of intervention and in anatomy, neurology, or even cardiology.

The latter makes it possible to train apprentice surgeons in very concrete clinical cases, and they are thus taken to an operating room to perform a sleeve gastrectomy; the apprentice surgeon is trained as closely as possible to real conditions, both by the realism of the environment and by the detail given to the patient's organs.

Virtual reality also opens up the field of possibilities in distance learning, and surgeons are sometimes obliged to cross the globe to learn a particular specialty; with this technology, very specific training becomes accessible anywhere and can promote exchange and collaboration between healthcare professionals from different countries.

Towards the democratization of virtual reality

While pioneers are trying to democratize the tool, virtual reality is still struggling to impose itself; the added value of this new tool would not yet be obvious to all practitioners.

The more patients and practitioners will test virtual reality, the more this technology will be adopted because support is very strong among those who have the opportunity to test this technology.

One thing is certain, little by little, we are crossing the boundaries of virtual, which is only the beginning, provided that virtual reality is accessible, easy to use, and has a wealth of content.

VR in Businesses

A technology emerges, and in a few months, it has become an essential need; it is often associated with video games; however, it is not only for being able to immerse yourself in an unusual world.

Companies use it regularly for marketing, training, and day-to-day work in their offices; it stood out in its early days as a technology in the service of recreation, but it is becoming ubiquitous as its capabilities are immense; attention, the immersion begins, welcome to a new universe for the greatest pleasure of your activity.

Virtual reality is making great strides.

This technology won the hearts of video game enthusiasts, and it allows you to immerse yourself in an environment fully; whether the experience is futuristic or realistic, users are very often amazed by the emotions generated, sometimes it is even almost impossible to tell the difference from reality; using a headset that fits in front of the eyes, users embark on extraordinary experiences.

Whether produced by brands like HTC, Sony, or even Oculus Rift, headsets are multiplying and are still very inaccessible to the general public because of their price; but the development of this technology aims to be of service to all shortly.

For the moment, the general public is not moving much towards this technology since the demand is focused on video games, which are still few; in fact, the fondest of virtual reality are businesses, they use it all over the place, whether it is to develop their business, to help consumers make their choice or even to train employees.

Companies are increasingly eager for this technology because they want to become innovative and not miss the boat; they use VR to raise awareness or train their employees; for the Volkswagen, BMW, and IKEA brands, it is a question of marketing through virtual reality.

This technology benefits from a wide range of possibilities for companies since it is a screen where images are broadcast and interactivity thanks to sensors to enter immersion; all sectors can take advantage of it and be part of the novelty.

Virtual reality, a technology to train employees

Virtual reality headsets are not for everyone, but on an enterprise-scale, it is proving to be a worthwhile investment, several software packages are now available to provide immersive experiences in the heart of businesses, but some do not yet have the use of these virtual reality headsets.

VR can be used for companies that have many employees and for which it is difficult to take charge of training or awareness, using one or more helmets, they can perform the experience when they have the time and the inclination; all this avoids reserving speakers, rooms, and slots to sometimes have no results because of the boredom generated by this type of event.

Thus, some large companies have chosen to invest in this innovation to help their employees; some companies have offered training on public speaking, the employee is then immersed and feels real conditions thanks to the helmet.

Fully immersed in a realistic universe, they then understand the issues of safety within their work. They are better able to listen than in a conference or meeting. Not only can such a tool help employees improve, but they also come into contact with technology at a generally low cost.

Virtual reality, a technology at the service of marketing

Another part of virtual reality is serving a business to win over customers, and that is why the VR market is starting to emerge; companies specialize in developing software to promote useful experiences in the course of a business.

In recent years, VR has had a big impact on the real estate industry; some agencies use virtual reality headsets to show clients around apartments; they can move around and observe the rooms as if they were there.

No more running around, which is an advantage for clients who do not have the time, and for busy real estate agents, this allows a first approach; the person visualizes the apartment before visiting it in real life.

In this same perspective, famous brands wanted to provoke immersion from a marketing point of view; IKEA plans to develop software for its customers, once their apartment has been reproduced identically using the software, they will be able to install furniture in their home using VR; the brand will have a marketing asset without any measure for the customer.

No need to move around and measure all the furniture at IKEA, all you need to do is immerse yourself in virtual reality; a user experience that will convince consumers all the more in their purchases; with this same concept, car brands also plan to create a virtual reality experience for the general public, people will be able to test a car through a helmet.

As a mini-booth, this type of marketing can occur anywhere, in a cinema, a shopping center, or an event; the immersion experience will convince possible future buyers.

In any case, VR is beginning to democratize in several sectors, whether for your employees or to promote your brand; everything becomes possible; an immersion gives emotions and is easier to convince as the person finds himself alone with himself.

Using this technology for your marketing or even your business is a major asset because it is efficient, and finally, on a business scale, the cost is lower; so why not try the experiment to train your employees on a future project or make them aware of the risks they run in their activity, the future is now, you might as well use it wisely.

VR market key players

Oculus VR, which became a subsidiary of Facebook after a buy-out for 2 billion euros in 2014, announced the availability of an API, "Passthrough API Experimental," allowing developers to create mixed reality applications by combining augmented reality elements with real-world elements; this makes it possible to add virtual elements to its real environment through the Oculus Quest 2 headsets.

Facebook: Facebook is thinking of having the solution with Horizon Workrooms, a remote collaboration application in virtual reality; it brings together up to 16 people in a virtual meeting room to discuss, share documents and make decisions.

HTC, Microsoft, Google, Sony, Samsung Electronics, Eon Reality, and a few others. It must be said that these different brands are currently dominating the market with their various products.

The Apple Company is one of them; indeed, she plans to launch a helmet already in preparation in 2022.

Even though VR investments are popping up worldwide, some countries have better potential than others; China, the Asian giant, tops the list.

In 2020 alone, it spent no less than $ 5.8 billion on VR technology; it must be said that this is a considerable amount; note that this figure represents about 30.8% of the total amount that should be spent on RVs worldwide.

In second place in the United States with $ 5.1 billion devoted to virtual reality, western Europe is in third place ahead of Japan with $ 3.3 billion.

How far can virtual reality go?

More and more used for training, recreation, or medicine, virtual reality is not a technology like the others: it is suspected of modifying our consciousness; Ethics specialists call for safeguards to be put in place.

Conditioning the soldiers

All over the world, academics like Erick Ramirez, but also content developers for virtual reality headsets, and consumer and employee protection agencies are starting to reflect on the ethical questions posed by virtual reality.

Simulation of the announcement by a manager of the closure of a factory to employees, treatment of phobias, video games, pornography, the uses of virtual reality is multiplying in laboratories of research, NGOs, companies, hospitals, homes, not to mention its use by the military.

Manipulate Consciousness

This enthusiasm is, of course, due to the drop in costs; it is now possible to acquire an autonomous virtual reality headset for less than 450 euros. However, these helmets are not for everyone; unprecedented powers are suspected if virtual reality interests many people.

Several phenomena are indeed activated during an immersive experience in virtual reality; in 2016, two German researchers from the Johannes Gutenberg University in Mainz, Michael Madary and Thomas Metzinger, sounded the alarm, Virtual reality can manipulate human consciousness," warns Thomas Metzinger for "Les Echos"; there is a risk that, within five to ten years, many people will become addicts.

All the academics questioned draw in the same direction: "No other technology has had the power to change us like this," worries Erick Ramirez, "Virtual reality is used to relieve pain or to treat phobias like that of spiders: it is proof that it can change our behavior," notes Guillaume Moreau, professor and researcher in computer science at Centrale Nantes.

Psychological trauma

Academics, like Michael Madary, Thomas K. Metzinger, or Erick Ramirez, begin to enact codes of conduct: "Any experiment considered unethical if it is carried out in real life, such as the simulation of 'rape or torture, should be banned in virtual reality,' says Erick Ramirez.

Same precautions with doctors "Virtual reality is not a magic wand that can be used any way you want to solve all problems: behind a phobia can hide a psychiatric pathology," warns Fanny Lévy, a psychiatrist at AP-HP and founder of the company MyReVe (virtual reality content to fight against fears).

CHAPTER 4:
AUGMENTED REALITY

Augmented Reality

Defining augmented reality (AR) is not that easy! Indeed, it is a transversal field that uses many different technologies; the very term augmented reality, which has appeared about "virtual reality," can be misleading; this is understandable enough since it is not "reality" that is augmented but our perception.

Augmented reality refers to digital methods that add to our perception of reality an overlay of contextual information in real-time.

Basics

Augmented reality can be seen as an interface between digital data, which will be described improperly as "virtual," and the real world; it is therefore different from virtual reality, to be clearer, it must have the following three characteristics:

Combine real world and real-time digital data

Be interactive in real-time with the user and the real world: a change in the real world leads to an adjustment of the digital layer.

Use a 3D environment.

These three points are more or less respected by the applications that are qualified as augmented reality. The Pokemon Go application has no interaction with the real environment other than retrieving data from the smartphone's gyroscope and compass; this is the "0" degree of augmented reality.

The real scenes are captured by a system and interpreted by a computing unit, a large part of the processing will consist of stalling and following the link between real and digital; to make glasses appear on your face, you have to know how to properly position your eyes, your nose, and of course in real-time.

Without calling into question the interest of these distinctions, it does not seem relevant to us to add new terms for the understanding of the field.

Indeed, in this representation, the distinction between AR and AV is very blurred, the introduction of Augmented Virtuality does nothing, and subsequently, we will no longer use this term.

Augmented reality allows data to be contextualized, that is, to place it in the right place; while many examples relate to vision, augmented reality can augment any of the five senses.

For the moment, 90% of augmented reality applications are visual, 4% are sound, and the traces that remain are mainly in research laboratories.

However, that touch may well be the next sense to be increased, if the tools are still in their infancy, the economic interest is not in doubt, imagine being able to touch the fabric of the sofa or clothing you want to buy online.

Mixed Reality, XR, and other buzzwords

For some time now, the concept of XR has also been developing, but the translation remains uncertain since some see it as an extended reality which encompasses AR and VR while others use the "X" to replace all the others, possible letters and therefore make it a synonym for immersive technologies.

AR history

Augmented reality is not about the future; there are already many, many applications and examples.

The concept of augmented reality is not new; indeed, Morton Heilig created in 1962 Sensorama a helmet equipped with a sensor to simulate a motorcycle ride in New York; even if this kind of application is more of virtual reality, that is to say, the possibility of visiting virtual universes, it contains the basic elements of augmented reality.

Another precursor, Ivan Sutherland, and his team will develop a head-up display (HUD) helmet that responds to head movements: the Damocles sword.

In the 1980s, Steve Mann was probably the first to offer an operational AR device, the EyeTap, a kind of headset allowing virtual information to be displayed in front of the wearer's eyes, and Steve will continue to develop this device to make it as light as a pair of glasses today.

The techniques

There are several techniques for making augmented reality; the bottom line is to locate the virtual concerning the real world.

Using geographic coordinates allows this location; augmented reality is often based on GPS data, which must be associated elements specifying the direction of vision; the internal compass and accelerometers provide additional data.

In this way, the augmented reality software can know where you are and which direction you are looking. It can display contextualized information.

Another way of knowing where you are can also be by recognizing an image or a pattern characteristic of augmented meaning, and we enter augmented visual reality through image recognition. The first markers used were simple monochrome and asymmetrical; they are still used today.

Newer computers and smartphones are powerful enough to process image recognition algorithms; markers can be classic images.

Augmented reality applications do not just recognize static images, they can analyze video streams, and this is how you can try.

It is also possible to recognize and track parts of the human body like the fingers, arms, legs, or even the whole, and we can think that in the fairly near future, all portable equipment will have this type of sensor and will therefore be able to increase the possibilities of interaction with the environment.

Augmented reality concepts

Augmented reality or its diminutive RA or AR in English is frequently used to designate an application allowing to visualize a virtual object, the latter being positioned on the surface that one is looking at, through his smartphone.

QR Code augmented reality.

But limiting augmented reality to this type of application is reductive given the many possibilities it offers; it is important to understand the concept well in order to seize its many possibilities as work, communication, or marketing tool.

Indeed, I prefer the term concept to technology because augmented reality is not ONE technology but rather the convergence of multiple software and hardware technologies to enrich our vision of reality.

Hud automobile

Be careful, and augmented reality is often assimilated or confused with virtual reality (VR), the difference should be noted: with augmented reality, users stay in touch with the real world, while virtual reality aims to transport them elsewhere, to another place.

This amalgamation certainly comes from the fact that we can broadcast virtual objects via augmented reality, its strength: enriching with information.

We human beings are endowed with five senses to perceive our environment, and if we want to increase it, we must succeed in enriching this perception with additional information or even make it interactive.

Senses

For smell, taste, and touch, it is difficult to decorate them, due to a lack of technology and ideas, some projects open a few doors for applications with exciting possibilities: a research group from UEC Tokyo has developed an interactive surface, called

"ClaytricSurface," the flexibility of which can be adjusted on-demand, but for the general public, it will still be necessary to wait a little bit.

For hearing, we note the use of audio guides, a very effective tool to complement a museum visit; they make it possible to enrich the textual information with an oral description, on request, which can be in the language of the visitor; this is one of the first forms of augmented reality: simple and effective.

But the evolutions of augmented reality are driven by all the new technologies; through the user's digital vision, it becomes possible to distribute information to them.

Visual information different forms

Text for description or legend

In 2D images such as photography, diagram, synthetic image

A 3D virtual object or scene, which integrates into real space.

Augmented reality captions

All this information can be contained in the application, but remotely if the device is connected, it can be static, giving us immutable information like the position of a mountain, or dynamic, coming from information from various sensors, remote or on-board.

But the most important and most interesting: this information clings to reality, fixing itself and following the movements of the objects we observe through our digital gaze.

Futuristic technology

Categorically no, the technologies used to implement an AR application are not new; they have been developed and refined for two good decades.

HUD Burst

The examples of operations are numerous and apply to various fields, and we can cite the, intended for military aviation, with all a range of information displayed such as trajectories, distances, Etc.

For the general public, using their webcam on their PC to display an object on their desk has long been achievable, but the interests of the clutter of his desk, especially mine, and the relative conveniences of setting up hamper imaginable scenarios.

The only factor that makes it accessible and usable now is the democratization of smartphones and tablets, small gems of technology of considerable power; they are connected, they integrate many sensors that tell us about the user's real environment: high definition camera, GPS, gyrometer, magnetometer, gravimeter, Etc. ; and finally, they can disseminate information.

AR 3 pillars

The first, your information: technical, educational, entertaining, advertising, your product, your scene, all of your media to broadcast.

The second is the means of dissemination; today, it is mostly because I just mentioned the smartphone screen, but it can also be by projection or diffusion on a glass plate.

Finally, the last pillar, the subject of our concerns, the user, we want to know its context, its situation, possibly its profile in the case of a commercial application, it is the context that will allow the information to be offered and displayed in an optimal, filtered manner; at from the point of view.

For any new project to create an AR application, an analysis based on these three pillars makes it possible to define the precise outlines and to set up specifications.

AR Common uses

The most common use of augmented reality, and the one that has made it known to the greatest number, is undoubtedly centered augmented reality; it consists of adding to a real marker, filmed by your webcam, your smartphone, or your tablet, a real-time 3D scene.

Usually, this scene is a simple 3D object that you can turn around; but we can imagine any kind of more or less complex 3D scene, static or animated, independent or interactive; in fact, anything you have seen in 3D can apply to this scenario, with a few scale constraints.

But if this use is perfectly suited for the presentation of a product or other model, its center of interest imposed by the marker does not increase our environment, this is where panoramic augmented reality comes in; augmented reality applications, we need to know where the viewer is located, and in which direction their observation is pointing; using GPS or other systems that allow us to triangulate its position, we geolocate it, and with the orientation sensors, we have enough information to enrich the panorama in front of it.

The strong impact of these uses did not escape the scenographers who quickly understood the educational and recreational value of augmented reality, and this has therefore been integrated into more or less complex interactive installations.

A frequent use in scenography, which derives directly from centered augmented reality, consists in increasing the video flow of a fixed camera in order to transform passers-by into actors or extras of a more or less interactive 3D scene.

AR added value

Today, most augmented reality applications have a playful approach because they arouse curiosity and are easy to practice.

They are widely used during trade shows or street marketing events and benefit from a second life beyond the event.

It is profitable from a marketing point of view and optimizes the investment because the shopper stays longer in contact with the product or the brand and easily shares the experience with those around him; in this context, it is better to assume its entertaining side without pretending to a practical application; it is through this that Ikea, in my opinion, has approached in the video its communication around its application:

By exploiting augmented reality, a company is positioning itself, at least in its communication, in digital innovation, with a large audience: the famous generation Y who is well over their twenties - sigh.

If augmented reality still makes it possible to differentiate yourself today, it will not last, at least not in this playful approach; like the web, things change quickly with AR.

AR Market Evolution

The near future is surely in the applications which apply to take the fundamentals of augmented reality again, that is to say when the information, the object, the product come to be registered interestingly in the reality of the user, and no longer when the object simply appears on a marker, in full screen, without further consideration of the context.

We help him to project himself with the product, and we encourage him by this process to get involved in this integration - and I dare to breathe: acquisition, then the interaction with the object becomes more natural because we are turning around; no need for a mouse, keyboard or landline; all that's left is the screen of the smartphone or tablet.

And that last screen barrier tends to disappear, manufacturers have understood that maintaining your smartphone remains the ultimate constraint and that you have to free your hands; we see the birth of augmented reality headset projects, thanks to Google Glass or other HoloLens (Microsoft), which allow information to be projected directly onto the lens of glasses, and there, we are no longer talking about research projects, but kits available to developers, to anticipate marketing to the general public.

Be aware that these headsets are not to be confused with virtual reality headsets like the Samsung Gear or the Oculus, which cut us off from reality and project us into a virtual world even though they are technologically close.

There remains the added value service in useful applications, which are not limited to presentation, but which are a help for the user, from the light application for cutting a cake into X parts, choosing the right size of the packaging box according to the volume of its shipment, passing on real-time information from its immediate environment; like smartphone apps, apps that provide a real service are the most successful.

This more practical reflection of AR, associated with the hands-free possibilities of AR headsets, opens up a wide field of applications in many areas: education, training, or just everyday work:

Imagine a tutorial for changing a car wheel, where the procedure is displayed directly on and around the wheel. OK, too simple, then for the human body?

Virtual Surgery

Augmented reality is in its infancy, and everything remains to be invented like the internet was in the 90s.

AR Basic principles

The principle of augmented reality is:

The presence of a camera that shows the content in real-time on the screen.

Sensor technologies that detect the precise location of the mobile terminal user, thanks to this geolocation, augmented reality pellets showing the surrounding points of interest appear on the screen.

The computing power integrated into mobile terminals, similar to a very powerful computer capable of propelling complex algorithms.

Technologies available

Augmented reality technologies all work on the principle of computer vision or "Computer Vision"; powered by complex algorithms, they detect distinctive elements in the real universe and then superimpose virtual content on it.

Tracking can be done with a marker, a visual, physical part usually in 2D that the computer is trained to recognize. The easiest solution to set up can also be done based on a 3D model but in a more controlled environment.

Actors in research

Until June 2015, three technologies stood out clearly: Vuforia, Wikitude, and Metaio, and this is not the case since Apple acquired the German company Metaio, specializing in augmented reality.

Vuforia:

Distributed by Qualcomm, Vuforia offers robust image tracking solutions but does not offer a correct solution for extended and tagless tracking.

Wikitude:

Wikitude offers a solution similar to its competitor Vuforia, with better-extended tracking or track without a marker.

Many players, such as the 44 screens agency, are also researching augmented reality techniques.

The pairs of augmented reality glasses

There are around forty pairs of glasses already on the market; the Augmented Reality site identifies and analyzes the augmented reality and virtual reality glasses and headsets.

Everyone has heard of Google Glass, a project almost dead - born, the new management of Google, has finally announced a new version 2.0 with a more professional destination for the next few months.

Epson Moverio

Since 2012, the Epson Company has been working on its augmented reality glasses and regularly improves them with the latest version, which appeared in June 2015.

This device differs from Google Glass by the fact that the display is stereoscopic; the user, therefore, has a virtual 3D rendering superimposed on the real world.

Hololens

Microsoft introduced in 2012 its pair of augmented reality glasses, which in its approach closely resembles Epson glasses; however, the term "Hologram" used by Microsoft is only a commercial term and does not provide a 3D projection in a real environment.

BMW

BMW more recently revealed a new pair of augmented reality glasses focused more on the general public. It is about augmenting the user's daily life with informative content.

Limits

The technological limits concerning augmented reality are mainly due to the equipment used; as we said, AR requires a lot of computing power that is not always found in smartphones, tablets, and even glasses on the market.

Despite the rapid evolution of these devices, they are not powerful enough to run very complex algorithms; the insufficient power of peripherals is felt, especially with augmented reality projects of monuments outside.

Indeed, technology is very sensitive to environmental changes: light color, brightness, weather changes, physical changes.

The technology is also difficult to implement when you want to increase a texture that looks too uniform, and it would be impossible to increase a smooth concrete wall.

Paired augmented reality glasses also experience the following issues:

Concern for the aesthetics and ergonomics of pairs of glasses requiring a pleasant device, light and compact and therefore expensive.

The display of content on spectacle lenses is not optimal; the screens are not entirely transparent, are too small but often much too thick, the field of vision and the display quality are severely limited.

Now that you know more about augmented reality and the differences between augmented reality and virtual reality find out all about virtual reality.

Aeronautics, automotive, defense, health rare are the sectors that escape this profound change that factory 4.0 represents today, among the technologies that are reshaping the world of industry: virtual reality and augmented reality; by immersing operators and machines in a digital environment, they allow the production chain to improve performance and become even more collaborative.

Virtual reality applications

Behind virtual reality and augmented reality, uses are based on the same principle: virtually modifying the environment where a user finds himself to offer him immersive or enriched content.

However, the experience offered by these two technologies is quite different.

Virtual reality is an immersive simulation of real or imaginary environments that relies on visual and auditory stimulation, and it is mainly used with headphones, augmented reality, on the other hand, allows superposition of the real world with a virtual one through digital tools such as a smartphone or connected glasses.

These tools, initially developed for the world of video games, are gradually establishing themselves in industrial mechanisms, their promise: the implementation of an industrial-scale virtualized environment that would improve performance and agility; focus on the benefits of these immersive technologies in the smart industry, and more particularly in the health sector.

Optimizing the design phases

The automotive industry pioneered virtual and augmented reality, some car manufacturers, such as Ford, for example, have created real immersion laboratories;.

Equipped with helmets, designers and engineers can examine all angles of their cars to different degrees and thus obtain more reliable, precise and better results; for them, this technique reduces the gaps between what is designed and what is achieved and also offers the possibility of optimizing time to market.

Virtual and augmented reality also has a huge role; products and manufacturing processes are becoming more and more complex for operators. Virtual assistance can thus become very useful in ensuring optimal control of the development of production.

Virtual reality is also a collaborative revolution. The virtual simulation will allow more stakeholders to validate the production chain: Even if we are 5,000 kilometers from each other, we will create a virtual collaboration area that will involve both experts non-expert audiences.

Better performance in production processes

In the factory, an optimized workstation is, in essence, a guarantee of performance for the operators and therefore of competitiveness for the company; thanks to virtual reality, it becomes possible to completely rethink its ergonomics in order to make it more efficient.

Thanks to simulation, we can quantify and assess the degree of the arduousness of certain positions in order to readjust certain elements and improve the working conditions of technicians.

Equipped with a headset, the user performs the assembly gestures of the parts. The software analyzes his posture in real-time and detects bad positions or overly complicated gestures; the results will allow an ergonomist to modify the tools' location to improve the fluidity of gestures.

In addition, at the end of the production line, the operator equipped with augmented reality glasses can be informed about the type of actions to be carried out to ensure the quality of the finished product, it becomes possible to add a contextual notice visible through augmented reality glasses which appears superimposed on the product, indicating step by step the last processes to be carried out.

Train through simulation

Virtual reality is also full of many benefits in terms of safety and training; thanks to it, it is in particular possible to simulate critical or dangerous situations for operators and machines, to know how to react in real cases; before being put to work in the field, technicians can thus be immersed virtually in their future work environment to be trained in possible dangers.

At its Sisteron site, Sanofi has launched initial training approaches using a digital 3D model of its workshops and production lines, operators can thus be certified and trained even before the factory is built; and for factories already operational, augmented reality can allow them to become more agile by supporting work processes.

Virtual and augmented reality can also be used in maintenance operations; if a component becomes dysfunctional in the production line, it must be repaired quickly; rather than having an expert come on-site, which can take a long time, we can now bring him in remotely.

While these new technologies create real opportunities in production activities, they require new skills and very specific know-how on the part of the employees concerned.

Companies wishing to make a successful transition to the 4.0 factory will therefore have to offer training modules adapted to operators already in place and consider recruiting new resources who have mastered these tools.

Challenges & Limitations of Augmented Reality

In 2017, virtual reality and augmented reality technologies experienced a meteoric expansion, with a 72% increase in the consumer market, for a total value of nearly $ 3.2 billion, the ARKit app, Apple's new framework that allows iOS developers to build augmented reality applications, alone had 375 million users in 2017.

Today, many professionals see augmented reality as a much greater potential than virtual reality; in about five years, AR should thus far surpass VR in terms of both users and content.

However, although increasingly used, primarily by businesses and individuals, augmented reality still has challenges to overcome to increase its performance and efficiency; GPS, for example, is only accurate to within 30 feet and hardly works indoors.

The human-machine interface

The first challenge is the reality access interface; smartphones are not the ideal interface: the screens are small, and the phone needs to be held at arm's length, limiting the user's freedom of action and movement.

More simply, having to download a specific application on your smartphone is one of the limits of augmented reality.

Currently, a new generation of devices such as Google Glass are enabling already more convenient use of augmented reality; shortly, it may be possible to play a computer game, or invite a friend over, put on their glasses, and play on the tabletop in front of you.

Over-information

Over-information is another of the limits of augmented reality; just as internet addiction is worrisome, over-addiction to augmented reality could mean people are missing out on what is right under their noses;.

Some people already prefer to use their smartphone applications rather than hiring an experienced guide, even if a guide can offer an interaction, experience and a personal touch not available in a mobile application.

Sometimes a simple plaque on the facade of a building is more efficient and cheaper than virtual information that can only be accessed by a few people with the right technology.

Confidentiality

The biggest challenge is that of confidentiality and social acceptance, image recognition technology, coupled with augmented reality, will make it possible to point our phones at people and instantly obtain information from their Facebook, Twitter, LinkedIn, or other online profiles.

Now, what would be your reaction if you see that the person you have just met already knows everything about your life and your background?

Promising future

Despite these concerns, the possibilities are endless; it will be possible to learn things about the city where you walk by simply pointing your phone at a building or monument.

It will be possible for those working in construction to save on materials by using virtual markers to designate the medium to be inspected.

Paleontologists working as a team to assemble a dinosaur skeleton could leave virtual "notes" for team members on the bones themselves; Doctors could superimpose a digital X-ray image of a patient on a mannequin for more realism.

AR advantages and disadvantages

Home asset

Augmented reality helps give reality a boost; indeed, it offers the possibility of projecting yourself into a new environment or offering you certain useful details; take the example of buying a new living room, with your smartphone or tablet, you can project what your new sofa would look like in your home, or even what your entire living room would look like.

Thus, augmented reality would give a whole new concept of online shopping; on a merchant site, this can create interactions that could never have existed between a customer and a seller.

Content enrichment

Augmented reality is a system for adding data, and it allows content to be enriched. It allows additional information to be provided in real-time in a defined situation or a specific environment, without the user's assistance, so he does not need to search for it: during a trip by car, during a tourist visit, or during a bike trip, for example, there are many advantages for users: culture, safety and time-saving in mind; augmented reality can become a personal assistant for each individual.

Social disadvantages

One drawback derived from such a breakthrough is the risk of a social dystopia; indeed, authors like Charlie Brooker often describe this situation with his series Black Mirror, based on new technologies and their contributions to life.

A recent report released by Accenture points out that a growing number of companies are taking advantage of "extended reality," a technology that includes virtual reality (VR) and augmented reality (AR), among others.

Entitled Waking Up to a New Realit, the report emphasizes the need to be aware of the opportunities of these technologies and the dangers they can represent; the authors say that in addition to posing dangers to privacy, extended reality also presents risks to mental health.

Like other key technologies in the digital revolution, the extended reality is valuable as it enables data to be collected and interpreted.

Applications running in AR, which combines natural and digital elements, can retrieve a multitude of information about their users, popular apps include Snapchat and Facebook, and can collect personal biometric data that can be used to identify us just by seeing our faces, other augmented reality apps can even record everything we see and hear.

Do we have all of these things in mind when we let our kids have fun with these kinds of apps? Suppose social media and app developers assure us that everything is secure and that our privacy is respected, in that case, there is no way of knowing exactly who has access to this information and what they do with it.

Personal data breaches are rife these days, the most trusted platforms on the surface present risks; the Facebook group, which recently acquired the virtual reality company Oculus and whose social network Instagram uses augmented reality, is also an important player.

When we use VR, we create and share data about our behavior and our movements in virtual environments that could one day imitate or even steal our identities; most virtual reality experiences are in video games, but new spaces for online socialization are developing thanks to VR.

The avatars that we develop to project ourselves into these virtual spaces will inevitably become linked to our real personality, thus offering even more data that can be collected and retrieved without our knowledge.

In addition, VR and AR are becoming more and more commonplace, and are now used for professional training, thus blurring the lines between the real world and the virtual world.

But extended reality presents other risks to our mental health. So far, research has not looked at this area, but we do know that Internet addiction is a very real problem for several people and concerns the massive use of social networks, especially young people.

The fusion of social networks and extended reality promises to offer us more immersive experiences, with the possibility of sharing our lives more and more online, but it could also make matters worse for people who use virtual space as a refuge from reality or who define their worth based on their number of likes or followers.

The important thing today, as these technologies continue to develop, is to ensure that they are deployed with due regard to the impact they may have on our daily lives and well-being.

These considerations should not be made after the fact to mitigate the damage, but well before the launch of these futuristic technologies.

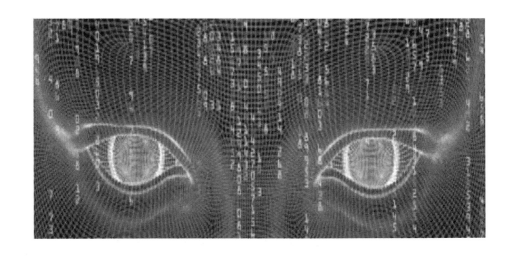

CHAPTER 5:
CONSPIRACY THEORY

Conspiracy theory

The conspiracy as an ideological system

The conspiracy as an ideological and symbolic system, the fear provoked by fictitious, imaginary or impossible to demonstrate plots, as well as the hypothesis of the existence of plots behind various historical events.

The denunciations of certain groups of influence or think - tanks, the expressions of various alternative beliefs, the phenomena of rumors, false information, political and religious extremisms, even certain critical approaches in the human and social sciences, thus form a heterogeneous whole in many cases summoned without distinction when 'it is about evoking the conspiracy theories.

A tool of social control

The variety of actors, ideologies, practices, and arguments to which the qualifier of conspiracy theory is appended testifies to its conceptual weakness, at least in certain uses, the extremely generic label of conspiracy theories is thus widely used as a mere disgraceful motive.

It aims to discredit or disqualify protest statements within the fields of power and the media, ultimately becoming a tool of social control.

Opposition to conspiracy theories stigmatizes and discriminates as much as it legitimizes established media, political or scientific institutions, it explains at little cost the mistrust and the oppositions they arouse or rather hides their root causes: poor representation, elite / people split, various forms of social exclusion, decline of supervision and socialization structures, aggravation social and economic inequalities, Etc.

Any attempt to understand or explain these phenomena, especially when it comes from the social sciences, is immediately largely brushed aside because it is part of a culture of excuse; this approach in terms of frontal opposition may appear, in certain aspects, as worrying as the productions it denounces.

Also, beyond conspiracy theories as such, it seems necessary to examine two aspects from a critical perspective, on the one hand, the discourses and uses of this infamous and qualifying labeling implemented by researchers from different disciplines of the human and social sciences.

On the other hand, the interactions between these divergent academic approaches and the media and political fields through the development of anti-conspiracy activism, which involves understanding the social conditions of emergence and the forms of mobilization.

The role of social networks in the inflation of rumors

At the time, several theories were listed, the first involved Chinese 5G networks; the radiation emitted by this frequency would have weakened the immune defenses of the population, hence the speed with which the epidemic would have spread.

However, Huawei had a research center in Wuhan, in short, the evil Chinese were punished for having taken the lead in cutting-edge technology, 5G transmitters have been regularly destroyed.

Another speculation attributed the epidemic to the P4 laboratory, which, in addition, had been created; couldn't there have been a top-level secret agreement to create a bacteriological weapon that would have eluded its designers, as in the myth of the sorcerer's apprentice?

This rumor had an anti-Semitic dimension which was analyzed, I pass on the miracle virtues of hydroxychloroquine, supposed to cure, according to the members, seriously affected patients and the whose only French government would have banned the use - because it was not expensive enough in the rest of the world, the epidemic was probably conquered thanks to the magic potion of Doctor Miracle.

The role played was highlighted, in these epidemics of interpretive delirium, by social networks, and on social networks, by people without any particular skills, but in whom confinement probably worsens pre-existing paranoid tendencies.

They manipulate: the vaccines they prepare in are part: putting a subcutaneous chip for everyone is NO, NO to Bill Gates' operations, NO to 5G ", yes, because there are people crazy enough to believe that the virus contains microchips intended to inform Bill Gates of our movements and maybe even our secret thoughts.

One in three Americans believes the Chinese created the coronavirus.

More than one in three Americans today believe the Chinese government has created the coronavirus as a weapon, another third is convinced that the health authorities in their country have exaggerated the threat of Covid-19, one in two Americans subscribes to one or the other of the conspiracy theories freely circulating on the internet.

And a team of psychologists from Atlanta has just released a study on which profiles are most likely to adhere to absurd theories, often inspired by science fiction, the belief that their government has information about visitors from another planet and maintains intimate relations with them.

A psychological ground favorable to conspiracy theories

There are typical profiles, and like that of the collector of injustice, he feels that he is being discriminated against, underestimated, and persecuted; killing takes revenge.

Several perpetrators of mass killings corresponded to this profile; People adopt conspiratorial beliefs to allay their feelings of injustice.

They believe they are regaining control through a meta-narrative that lends the appearance of overarching meaning to facts they are unable to understand rationally.

Such a profile is impulsive and considers everyone else to be naive who get fooled by what he calls the official narrative; an excess of doubt provides psychological ground for conspiracy theories.

People who feel that scholars are mistaken or corrupt, that experts are knowingly lying, that the authorities are fooling them in order to increase their power, are also those who most readily adhere to nonsense gleaned from the internet, diffusing doubt is a formidable weapon, and how the tobacco companies have used this provision to deceive consumers for decades.

As early as the 1950s, indisputable medical studies had established the extraordinary danger of smoking and its determining role in the proliferation of lung cancer; realizing that smokers did not want to believe that their habit was killing them, the major American tobacco companies published counter-studies.

They expressed doubts about the results obtained by the doctors, and the subliminal message was: there are a lot of different opinions, so you do not have to worry about it, we are taking care of it, yes, doubting everything often leads to believing in anything.

Conspiracy theories have always existed; over time, they have diversified and globalized; the internet, which experienced rapid development in the early 2000s, seems to have played a major role by offering them a large showcase.

For historians, the attacks of September 11, 2001, constitute a key event in the development of modern conspiracy theories, of which the United States is very often the target, the invasion of Iraq in 2003 probably helped amplify the phenomenon, with state lies and real plots providing fertile ground for conspiracy theories.

For the last decade, the development of social networks has further accentuated their visibility and increased their scope; there are hundreds of them today, from the classic to the wackiest.

These theories are based partly on false information, the famous fake news; in 2018, a team of MIT researchers succeeded in showing that fake news was 70% more likely to be shared than true news, especially on Twitter.

The reason would be as follows: they arouse more emotions such as surprise, a feeling of novelty, fear, or disgust; moreover, fake news of a political nature spreads three times faster than others, with all the consequences one might imagine.

Daily conspiracies

We are all confronted with conspiracy theories daily, and distinguishing right from wrong takes time and skill; we recently realized how much energy it took when we decided to play the game during the lockdown, where we regularly received conspiratorial videos via social media.

Conspirators do not believe in chance.

Conspiracy theories are that they often confuse correlation with cause and effect, a correlation between two phenomena can be due to chance or to a cause common to both phenomena, but conspirators generally do not believe in chance; rather, they believe that everything is linked, organized, and planned by malicious people with much power, like politicians, scientists, or businessmen like Bill Gates.

They also do not believe in coincidences; certain theories have thus suggested that the Covid-19 would have appeared because of 5G, those who spread those used maps that claimed to show a correlation between the development of 5G in certain regions and the appearance of the coronavirus, especially in large metropolises like Wuhan.

The first problem, it has been shown that some had used fake cards that did not show the 5G network, but the fiber-optic network, second problem, the first tests of 5G date back about two years before the appearance of Covid-19; next to that, it makes sense that this virus and 5G both developed mostly in populated areas.

Population density could therefore explain that there is a certain correlation between the two in places, which does not mean that 5G is at the origin of Covid-19; according to this logic, we could say that the level of pollution in the air is the cause of the epidemic since there is more pollution and contamination in the big cities.

What should hold our attention?

Several other elements should hold our attention when confronted with a conspiracy theory, the worldview is often fatalistic and pessimistic, and the people who propagate them do not focus on constructive solutions to fix the problems.

It may explain that people who defend conspiracy ideas have a hard time arguing and accepting any point of view.

They have a form of obsession with their ideas and do not show much mental flexibility; while seeking to convince, they are persuaded to hold the truth and to be initiated into a hidden knowledge to which others do not have access, there is, therefore, a form of esoteric dimension in some conspiracy theories, as can be seen in sectarian religious movements.

Moreover, critical thinking is presented as an essential virtue, so it is only used in one direction.

People who believe in conspiracy theories consult fact-checking sites and are very critical of the traditional so-called mainstream media, but they are not at all with the conspiratorial media which they consult extensively.

They are therefore victims of a powerful confirmation bias by locking themselves into a media universe limited to the internet and often only consider information that is relevant to them to be valid.

Research has also shown that conspirators often have fairly low self-esteem, are unhappy with their lives, and believe the system is the cause of their problems, this feeling of possessing the truth, and the need to become right then a means of valuing oneself, like a kind of revenge, the communities that develop around conspiracy theories also provide support and a sense of belonging.

We can see it in the USA in groups who believe that the earth is flat, who show themselves united on the internet or through the organization of meetings.

Psychologists have also found that conspirators often confuse cause and consequence and believe that there can be no major consequences without a major cause.

For them, the effects of the current pandemic are so great that it can only be the work of a huge conspiracy to harm the world's population; in the same vein, if in 2015 Bill Gates mentioned the risks of a possible future pandemic, it is that he orchestrated the one we know today.

Finally, one method that can be used to detect and challenge conspiracy theories is to point out their many contradictions, and one will try to convince us that Covid-19 does not exist while the other will explain to us that this virus is no more dangerous than the flu.

One will tell us that global warming is a hoax and the other will try to show us that the pandemic is an organized plot to reduce the world's population in order to reduce global warming.

Difficult to find consistency, the reality is that these theories are riding on our ignorance, our uncertainties, and our anxieties.

They also surf on the uncertainties of scientists who have to deal with a new phenomenon that takes time to be studied and understood, but where conspiracy theories seek to impose certainties and offer simple answers to a complex situation, science advances in small steps and always leaves room for questioning;

it is now up to us to give ourselves the means to be able to distinguish between the two.

COVID-19

Disease emerged in a Wuhan city that hosts a level 4 laboratory, a type of highly secure laboratory in which dangerous viruses are handled; more specifically, this institution accidentally escaped and started the pandemic.

No evidence has been shown to support this theory, and natural origin still seems the most likely.

The problem is that the investigation is stalling; in early 2021, the WHO mission was dispatched to China to investigate the virus 's origin.

Pandemic start

It is a crucial question that we do not yet know how to answer; from the start, in December 2019, experts favored the hypothesis of species skipping, that is, that of a virus present in an animal that suddenly becomes capable of infecting humans; this is how the SARS epidemic started, for example, as well as many influenza epidemics.

Attention soon turned to a market in Wuhan, stocked with exotic animals that could have helped transition the virus; the pangolin was initially considered a potential intermediate host, as a coronavirus genetically similar to SARS-CoV-2 has been isolated from the species.

Finally, the coronaviruses detected in market animals were too far genetically from SARS-CoV-2 for this thesis to be validated, no convincing animal host has therefore been found yet.

But according to a new study published in Scientific Reports, more than 47,000 wild animals have passed through the Wuhan market in the 2.5 years preceding the first case of COVID.

Like any emerging virus, SARS-CoV-2 likely caused a few scattered cases first, without subsequent transmission, kind of like a wet firecracker that goes out on its own.

According to an article published in Science, it was probably between mid-October and mid-November 2019 that the first human-to-human transmissions took place; at one point, an infected person transmitted the virus to several others, and it was in December that the number of cases started to be large enough to attract attention.

The Yunnan track

One lead seems privileged: the ancestor of SARS-CoV-2 could be a bat coronavirus; after the first cases broke out, Wuhan Institute of Virology scientist Shi Zhengli spotted several bat viruses closely related to SARS-CoV-2 that had been collected over the previous 15 years; the closest, named CoV RaTG13, about 96% identical to the newcomer, was isolated in 2013 from horseshoe bat guano in Yunnan province.

Surprisingly, six miners working in the area contracted pneumonia in 2012 - three died from it, a medical thesis had been devoted to their case and resurfaced in the media; in November 2020, a Chinese team confirmed this story in Nature, explaining that this is what triggered the cave sampling in 2013.

Researchers and WHO doubts

At the start of the pandemic, the hypothesis of an accidental leak was quickly ruled out; in February 2020, a group of about 30 scientists published in The Lancet a letter strongly condemning conspiracy theories suggesting that COVID-19 does not have a natural origin.

In June 2021, however, ABC News reporters reported that several of the letter's signatories reconsidered their position and believe that an accidental origin is, in fact possible, separately, a June article reveals that the letter's initiator had undisclosed scientific and financial ties to the Wuhan Institute of Virology.

On the WHO side, the accident thesis is not completely dismissed either; an international team was sent to China by the organization from January 14 to February 10, 2021, on the virus trail, in collaboration with Chinese scientists.

Direct transmission of the virus through a reservoir animal is considered probable by the report's authors, while the laboratory accident is considered extremely unlikely.

However, the director of the WHO called for a new investigation with specialized experts on an accidental leak of the virus, noting that the experts sent to China struggled to gain access to raw data.

As scientists with relevant expertise, it is necessary and possible to make more clarity on the origins of this pandemic, we need to make hypotheses about natural and laboratory origins seriously until we have sufficient data .

In an article re-published on the BioRxiv platform, the American researcher explains that having recovered 13 sequences saved in Google Cloud, they correspond to infections that occurred very early, before the cases detected at the Wuhan market, and therefore to strains of the virus closer to the initial bat virus; early viral strains are crucial in understanding the chronology of virus mutations.

US intelligence reveal

In January 2021, the US State Department issued a memo, according to which several researchers from the Wuhan Institute of Virology fell ill in November 2019 and were hospitalized with symptoms similar to those of COVID-19 or seasonal illness, few details are available, especially on the type of research carried out by these scientists.

Accident scenarios

The idea that a virus deliberately created by Chinese scientists, endorsed by former United States President Donald Trump and circulated in early 2020 in conspiracy circles, has helped discredit the laboratory accident hypothesis.

The accident thesis covers a whole spectrum of possibilities; it could have been a simple sample of the virus from a bat in the field that led one of the researchers to become infected.

He reportedly brought the virus back to Wuhan without knowing it; it could also be a security breach that caused one of the samples stored at the laboratory to be accidentally "released" outside somehow.

Finally, and this is considered the least likely lead, the virus could have been created in the laboratory as a result of genetic modifications of a natural bat virus.

We know that scientists at the Institute were working on gain-of-function experiments, which aim to increase the transmissibility of certain viruses to understand the mechanisms of infection better.

Does SARS-CoV-2 have any weird features?

In the spring of 2020, many experts suggest that if the virus had been created in the laboratory, there would be traces of genetic manipulation in its genome.

However, according to other researchers, the structure of the SARS-CoV-2 genome does not exclude any hypothesis.

In addition, some characteristics of SARS-CoV-2 intrigue scientists, note once again that a natural evolution of the virus can also explain these traits.

First of all, this virus has a very strong ability to attach itself to human cells; from its emergence in December 2019, it is highly contagious and very suitable for ACE2 receptors, which allow it to enter our cells.

In general, this adaptation to humans is done in stages and takes time, some researchers are finding that the virus resembles its cousin responsible for SARS as it was in late 2003 after many months of evolution.

Then, the S protein of SARS-CoV-2, which allows it to attach to human cells, has a kind of lodge well suited to a human enzyme, called furin.

This enzyme binds to protein S and cuts it in half, making it active and able to fuse with the cell membrane; this step is essential for the virus to enter cells; however, no coronavirus with an S protein that is genetically more than 40% identical to that of SARS-CoV-2 has this furin cleavage site.

The "manual" insertion of this site, through genetic manipulation, is not to be ruled out even though there is no evidence to support this thesis at this point.

According to many researchers, Nature does not need human help to make viruses with such pandemic potential, and naturally, within a host like a bat, coronaviruses can swap pieces of the genome and transform quickly, just as influenza viruses do; to this day, the enigma remains unresolved, and the detailed history of this coronavirus may never be fully traceable.

Filter bubbles

The filter bubbles are the result of this new media and, essentially, digital ecosystem, and some communities are juxtaposed with each other on social networks in particular.

The filter bubble is at the same time this informational, communicational, and ultimately social confinement in a kind of community that operates in a vacuum, where some information enters, and others does not.

The filter is first of all your clicks, your preferences, which are sorted according to fairly complex algorithms by social networks and search engines, which mean that you always find information that goes in the direction of what you have, searched before and your preferences.

There is a self-reinforcement of our own beliefs, convictions because the information is tailor-made sorted.

Anyone can experiment with it on non-political, economic, or social subjects, after buying a pair of shoes online, without ad blockers or anti-trackers; in the following day's shoe advertisements appear on the sidelines of the pages you visit.

It is about personalizing the information presented to you; when it comes to conspiracy information, the more you search for conspiratorial information, the more access you have to conspiratorial information.

Many people ask the same questions; on social networks, a community effect is created where people confirm their beliefs, feed them, maintain them among themselves.

This informational and communicational confinement becomes social because your own marginal, heterodox, sometimes absurd beliefs can cut you off from your relationships in the physical world.

On the internet, you then find a community of sharing, a community of thought that can sometimes become friends, and this is evidenced by what the patients live, a community which thinks that the earth is flat, whose beliefs are extreme and marginal, and whose members often encounter difficulties in their family relations, sometimes even leading to divorce; there are therefore dating sites for plates which reinforce this confinement from which it is difficult to escape.

We are subject, to be right or to read articles that go in our direction, the important thing is to know; we can reason with ourselves quite easily by making the effort of a critical approach.

Often conspiracy theorists present themselves as people who see beyond, who doubt; this critical approach is healthy and the basis of all scientific research, but we still have to go to the end.

You should not doubt everything except the conspiracy hypothesis as they do, it is possible to encourage non-systemic conspirators that are to say not yet totally convinced that the conspiracy constitutes the alpha and the omega of social relations to cross their sources of information, to mix the types of informational supports, also in ideological terms to have all the available arguments and to get a more objective or documented idea.

What is more difficult is in the case of a radicalized individual, convinced that the plot is everywhere; in his social bubble, he had to give up a lot, he would then have to take this path of social disaffiliation a second time to renounce his beliefs; however, this work is tedious and does not guarantee that all that has been lost will be found.

Another response can be made to break through these filter bubbles: education in the media, media criticism, criticism of sources of information and documentation, we have been talking about it for 20 years, and unfortunately, it remains wishful thinking; this requires structural adjustments: teacher training, the establishment of dedicated school programs, Etc.

How can scientists respond to conspiracy theories?

First of all, some scientists are tempted by or themselves carriers of conspiracy theories, so it is hard to say that we are immune and can authoritatively answer as scientists.

That being said, scientists in so-called hard sciences are beginning and must get used to seeing their expertise challenged by pseudo-physicians, pseudo-physicists, pseudo-biologicals, Etc.

They must therefore do educational work to explain their Science, their research processes, their methodology, their results, and the fact that complexity is necessary to understand phenomena that are themselves complex.

To take the example of the Platonists, one of their arguments is that of the obvious: when the weather is nice, I see houses several hundred kilometers away, it is because the earth is flat, it is then up to researchers to explain that there are counterintuitive things, multifactorial phenomena. Immediate common sense is not necessarily scientific truth.

In the human and social sciences, more accustomed to questioning their expertise, it is a question of understanding how many individuals come to adhere to a theory that was until then marginal.

We must understand the societal environment, the mistrust of the dominant, the media, politicians for often justified reasons and not ridiculing them at the risk of reinforcing their confinement and accentuating mistrust.

We must not only do anti-conspiracy activism or stigmatization work, we must return to the basis of the social science approach, understanding, not to be confused with a so-called culture of excuse, seeking to understand the conspiracy phenomenon as a whole has been a subject of study since the 1950s and 1960s in the United States, but it is relatively new in the French-speaking world: since the 2010s.

It is new research that needs to be developed to investigate anti-vaccine phenomena, anti-Semitic or anti-Masonic movements today, and this requires careful and careful analysis.

We now know how these theories are born, how they circulate, what are the privileged scapegoats, the factors, and certain determinants of adherence to these theories, Etc.

Based on this detailed diagnosis, the social sciences can provide answers to the public authorities, which must implement them, in particular, to educate the media and improve the democratic participation of citizens.

It is a question of proposing ethical practices of democratization to the democratic regimes, and thus diverting individuals who ask themselves real or sincere questions about the dysfunctions of our regimes and who, in part of them, twist towards speeches, if criticism of the dominant is not bad in itself, on the contrary, conspiracy is a form of pseudo accusatory and victimizing criticism that requires being.

How is AI making us all paranoid?

There is a tendency to praise the merits of AI, to imagine a promising future for it made up of killer robots, super-intelligence, and augmented humans.

First of all, artificial intelligence is overused to give an idea, "the most successful artificial bits of intelligence have less common sense than rats.

Moreover, the various scandals in recent years tend to fuel public mistrust, and it is difficult to distinguish true from false in the practices of the major digital players.

According to researchers and associations, the phones cannot be tapped, it is not over; social networks themselves play an important role in accelerating conspiracy frenzy through their recommendation algorithms, breaking down the last barrier to mental health.

Conspiracy is a kind of resignation of thought, and it is going to find someone else who would explain everything; we are certain of everything, there is no longer any need to think, you abandon yourself to the other; To doubt everything or to believe everything, these are equally convenient solutions, both of which dispense us from thinking.

The digital world pushes humans towards paranoia.

Science leaves no room for nuance, whether it is right or wrong, the knowledge of science is essentially paranoid, 2 + 2 = 4, that is certain.

Conspiracy provides definitive answers where humans cannot find them; it is no longer a question of critical thinking, on the contrary; It is a phenomenon of credulity: we want to believe.

We can ask ourselves whether it is worth creating a completely paranoid society about AI programs that do not work well?

How do conspiracy theories emerge and fall apart?

The Illuminati and Reptilians control the highest levels of government, NASA willfully hides evidence from the Flat Earth, the US military is conducting experiments on aliens in Area 51, the SARS-CoV-2 coronavirus has escaped from a Wuhan laboratory, 5G allows the spread of disease.

All of these theories have one thing in common: they are conspiracy theories, but how do they emerge?

How is their narrative framework constructed?

And how do they differ from real conspiracies?

Recently, using artificial intelligence, a team of American researchers shed some light on the dynamics of conspiracy theories.

A new study by UCLA researchers offers a new way to understand how baseless conspiracy theories emerge online; research combines sophisticated gene editing and in-depth knowledge of folklore.

The authors illustrated the difference between the narrative elements of a debunked conspiracy theory and those that arose when journalists covered an actual event in the media.

A veritable conspiracy - and the spread of misinformation about the 2016 Pizzagate myth, a conspiracy theory that a Washington DC pizza place was the center of a child sex trafficking ring.

AI can automatically reveal all the people, places, things, and organizations in a story disseminated online, whether real or fabricated and identify how they relate to each other.

Whether it is a conspiracy theory or an actual story, the narrative framework is established by the relationships between the storyline elements.

Building on the huge amount of data available on social media, and thanks to improvements in technology, systems are increasingly able to learn to 'read' stories, almost as if they were human.

They tend to fall apart easily

Visual representations of these story frames showed researchers how false conspiracy theory narratives are held together by threads that connect multiple people, places, and things, but they found that even if just one of those threads was cut, the other pieces often could not make a cohesive story without it.

If you remove one of the characters or story elements from a conspiracy theory, the connections between the other pieces of the story break down.

Stories around real conspiracies, because they are true, tend to hold together even if a given piece of the story is taken out of the frame.

Take the example of Bridgegate, even if several threads had been removed from media coverage of the scandal, the story would have stood: All of the characters involved had multiple points of connection due to their roles in New Jersey politics.

To analyze the Pizzagate, in which the conspiracy theory was born from a creative interpretation of pirated emails published in 2016 by Wikileaks, the researchers analyzed nearly 18,000 messages from April 2016 to February 2018 from discussion forums on the Reddit and Voat sites, the data generated by the AI analysis allowed researchers to produce a graphical representation of the narratives, with layers for the main subplots of each story, and lines connecting key people, places and institutions to inside and between these layers.

In this conspiracy, we found that the rest of the connections do not hold up if you remove Wikileaks as one piece of the story.

The rapid emergence of conspiracy theories

Another difference between real and false stories concerns the time to construct them; narrative structures around conspiracy theories tend to build and stabilize quickly. In contrast, narrative frameworks around actual conspiracies can take years to emerge.

The Pizzagate narrative framework stabilized a month after the Wikileaks reveal. It has remained relatively consistent over the next three years.

Tangherlini says it is increasingly important to understand how conspiracy theories abound, in part because stories like Pizzagate have inspired some to take action that puts others at risk, threat stories found in conspiracy theories may involve or present strategies that encourage people to take action in the real world, Edgar Welch went to this Washington pizzeria with a gun looking for caves believed to be hiding victims of sex trafficking.

UCLA researchers also wrote another article examining the narrative frameworks surrounding COVID-19 conspiracy theories.

In this study, which was posted to an open-source forum, they follow how conspiracy theories are superimposed on previously circulated conspiracy theories, allowed the birth of new conspiracies, such as the idea that 5G cellular networks spread the coronavirus.

Researchers have developed an AI capable of distinguishing between conspiracy theories and real conspiracies that are very real.

It will be possible to fight very effectively against fake news spread very easily and quickly on social networks; it is because of the fake news that Twitter is testing a feature to dissuade its users from liking false information.

Researchers have developed an AI capable of meeting this challenge; after presenting the artificial intelligence of the chatbot to speak with the dead, here is that of the artificial intelligence specializing in the fight against conspiracy theories.

Conspiracy theories are not as complex as actual conspiracies.

Like the artificial intelligence that determines the age category of a film by reading its script, this new AI analyzes accounts from conspiracy theories such as those of QAnon, Pizzagate, and the Illuminati.

Then she compares them with real stories that strongly resemble conspiracies; the peculiarity of this artificial intelligence is that it can retrieve the necessary information from forums or from Twitter which is the most popular platform for spreading conspiracy theories.

In addition, artificial intelligence identifies different people, but also all objects and places that are mentioned in conspiracy theories as well as those of conspiracies.

UCLA researchers were thus able to make some interesting discoveries; first, they explained that conspiracy theories mostly have choppy narratives and fewer actors, generally speaking, the more information there is, the more coherent conspiracy theories become; on the contrary, this is when the real conspiracies gain momentum.

In short, a conspiracy theory never reaches the complexity of a real conspiracy; as the researchers said, this artificial intelligence could prove very useful for forums and social medi.

It could be implemented to notify users when fake news is circulating, for now, researchers are planning to make artificial intelligence even more autonomous; she could verify the information shared by conspiracy theories and conspiracies herself.

Six avenues to understand the conspirators

Disillusionment, anguish, isolation, anger, and mistrust of authorities are many reasons why sane people can adhere to conspiratorial theories in times of crisis. Experts say, good news, it is possible to help them get through this long as you avoid judgment and confrontation.

Beyond prejudices

Forget the stereotype of the angry young white man who sub-scribes to trash radios; there is not a typical conspirator since this phenomenon affects people with very diverse profiles.

The trend has been stable since June 2020: 20% of respondents maintain a so-called conspiratorial view of the world; it is much higher than expected, and it is worrying because it reflects a significant erosion of trust in the authorities.

Among the conspirators are as many men as women, and as many rural as urban, the main difference is education, one-quarter (24%) of conspiracy theories have at most a high school diploma, while 13% have a university degree; the 25-44-year-olds are also more represented.

Unsurprisingly, they are ready to set fire to 5G cell towers. Adherence to certain theories varies a lot from one individual to another; some are less extremist. They feel that the government is hiding information from them, and mistrust has set in.

The expression of distress

A pandemic is terrible for morale, and humans have all kinds of strategies to avoid drowning - including cutting themselves off from reality.

The anxiety burden associated with the crisis is so severe that they defend themselves by denying the existence of COVID-19 or by downplaying its health consequences.

How you react to hard knocks depends a lot on your past, someone who has experienced social rejection and who, therefore, does not feel a belonging to the community may have the reflex to shun the authorities' message in order to adhere to conspiratorial discourse, observes the professor at UQAM, often, it is not so much the ideology that appeals to the person as the idea of finally being part of a group, no matter which one.

The pandemic is a disinformation incubator, served on a silver platter to anxious people who spend far more time than usual on the web.

The same goes for the past year; the organization's workers have received a record number of calls from people distraught because a loved one has become a conspirator.

Isolation seems to have accentuated membership in marginalized groups, notes the trained sociologist; as many seek alternative social circles, the leaders of extremist groups rely on this to recruit: they offer a surrogate family, united by common beliefs, as well as social activities, such as demonstrations.

Betrayed by science

One day, the mask is worth nothing to protect against COVID; the next day, everyone must wear it in the shops, one day, such a vaccine is deemed safe, and the population is urged to receive it; the next day, its distribution was suspended following a further notice.

This hesitation of science is nothing new researchers often disagree, and this is how knowledge advances, but the general public has never been so exposed to their struggles as this year, and that unsettles many people.

The health crisis has made us lose faith in an all-powerful science, holder of the truth, and this distressing revelation has provoked in some a rejection of the scientific discourse carried by the competent authorities, now considered with suspicion; subscribing to parallel explanations gives them the feeling of not being bamboozled by official voices and, in the end, they have the illusion of regaining some control over their lives disrupted by COVID.

It is the brain's fault.

If many people embrace conspiratorial ideas, it is also difficult to defend themselves against false information. These are real mental sweets, and education helps develop critical thinking and reasoning skills, prevents falling into certain traps, but does not completely immunize against false stories.

No need to try to make a conspirator listen to reason; it would lead to a dialogue of the deaf, especially since the pandemic is a disinformation incubator, served on a silver platter to anxious people who spend far more time than usual on the web; giving it a competitive edge.

It must be said that the authors of misleading information cultivate the art of titillating attention, by relying on the effect of surprise or fear, argues the sociologist, "Since the content is often consistent with our intuitions, the information seems plausible to us.

The worst part is that once stored between the two ears, it is very difficult to deconstruct it because it is an expensive activity for the brain, which is rather stingy with its energy.

To add another layer, being exposed to information contrary to our beliefs puts certain brain modules on the alert as if we were under attack in our identity which is why we care so much about the vision of the world to which we subscribe.

How to reach out to a conspirator

Hearing your sister or best friend convey ideas that you find delusional is a painful experience; we can feel incomprehension, disappointment, and frustration with this loved one we thought we knew, better to maintain contact.

However, if possible, Otherwise, once cut off from their basic social circle, which offered them other perspectives on the world, the person is likely to become more involved.

Usually, people who buy conspiracy theories have made their choice; they have learned a lot and have a coherent discourse in their eyes.

So any ideological confrontation is sterile, »You can keep the dialogue open by avoiding topics that are likely to get out of hand, and instead focus on the emotional connection by discussing the feelings that the person has had since the start of the crisis, what is happening at work, or by evoking common memories.

But you have to try to distinguish the person from the ideas they profess and show them that you care about them even if you do not share their views at all.

Conspiracy theory claims the Internet has been 'dead' since 2016

A conspiracy theory claim that the Internet has been dead for several years and that much of the content on it has been created by bots; some American media have recently highlighted this fanciful assumption.

The Earth would be flat, the coronavirus vaccines would contain 5G microchips, and these are some of the most bizarre and sometimes dangerous conspiracy theories circulating on the Internet.

According to this conspiracy theory, the web has not existed for several years, and a good part of the content published on the web, including the lines you are reading now, would have been produced by robots.

Where did this theory come from?

Journalist Kaitlyn Tiffany, the author of the investigation published in the Atlantic on August 31, 2021, first learned about the theory on an English-language online discussion board, Agora Road's Macintosh Café, an exchange platform originally devoted to the culture of vaporwave, an artistic movement that refers in particular to a genre of electronic music. Users sometimes discuss conspiracy theories there.

The dead internet postulate was first developed in a lengthy text published on January 5, 2021, by a user who pretends that much of the Web is Wrong.

The anonymous author told The Atlantic that he is an operations supervisor for a logistics company in California, in the western United States.

Users originally wrote the theory he describes in his post of other online chat platforms, he explains.

What does this theory say?

According to this theory, the internet network would be dead in 2016 or 2017; by dead, the author of the message published on the forum means that the web seems empty and devoid of any human and entirely sterile.

It should be noted that the postulate is rather disjointed; the author of the post mentions artificial intelligence networks, in other words, robots, which operate in collaboration with secret influencers paid by people who are not named.

They are believed to be behind a large part of the supposedly human-produced content published on the Internet.

Their goal would be to create consumers who will purchase a growing range of newly standardized cultural products.

The Internet user still delivers several elements which, according to him, would allow supporting his theory; thus, users with whom he was in contact, on the Internet, have all evaporated without leaving any trace; and, the same photos and the same responses posted over and over again over the years.

The dead internet theory is a niche among conspiratorial ideas; although it has caught on, a video in Spanish dedicated to the subject and published on the YouTube platform has been viewed more than 260,000 times since May 2021.

Why is it wrong?

The Internet is not dead, and not all of the content you find there is created by machines; on the other hand, much content on the Internet is made by robots.

In 2020, 40% of global internet traffic originated in bot activities; according to US cybersecurity firm Imperva, a bot is a software operating autonomously and automatically.

In detail, 25.6% of these bots were described as malicious, and 15.2% as benevolent.

What are these bots doing?

Some are chatbots; conversational robots used to provide information to Internet users in an automated manner.

Some of these bots are also used to spread false information or create deepfakes, very realistic videos but entirely artificial and often used for malicious purposes.

If they do exist, all of which does not mean that the conspiracy theory of the slow Internet is realistic.

Simple conspiracy theory or real conspiracy

While the effects of conspiracy theories and fake news led to deadly consequences in Washington, researchers have developed artificial intelligence to disentangle the truth from the false.

Faced with the proliferation of fakes news and conspiracy theories on social networks and their direct consequences on society, researchers at the University of California at Los Angeles (UCLA) have succeeded in developing an artificial intelligence allowing distinguishing what is true from what is not.

To do this, this AI takes its ground where conspiracy theories are born: social networks and online forums. It brings together all the conspiracy/conspiracy publications published there; every sentence from every post is dissected and categorized in terms of 'subject, verb, and complement.

AI identifies the authors of these posts and the actors, places, and supposed facts that they imply.

Ultimately, AI distinguishes between the fake and the real, not perfect; it enjoys human intelligence support. Researchers also analyze certain elements of the stories, their sources, and how they are constructed.

What sets them apart?

By analyzing conspiracy theories and proven conspiracies, the creators of AI have come to several conclusions.

Conspiracy theories have a small number of actors, each of which is of major importance; conversely, real conspiracies tend to involve a much larger number of people.

Likewise, conspiracy theories carry very little information, and they are essentially based on a handful of elements, which makes them easily understandable and, de facto, more popular; in general, real conspiracies involve an infinite amount of information, which accumulates over time.

Conspiracy theories, based on few actors and little information, take shape very quickly; this is what makes them go viral on the Internet; the theory is built on very few elements, it is understood quickly, it spreads at lightning speed; conversely, actual conspiracies are regularly uncovered and take time to solidify.

Typically, for a conspiracy theory to emerge and become popular, it needs to be based on a few elements that have a basis of truth; the researchers say these elements are then deceptively linked to each other by a few storytellers form a story.

Since the dawn of time, people have liked to share stories that allow them to explain phenomena that go beyond them; today, social networks accelerate the sharing of these myths: they spread very quickly and, therefore, gain credibility with those who are sensitive to them.

Concrete case

To explain the construction of conspiracy theories, Professor Vwani Roychowdhury, interviewed by Spectrum News, took the example of one of the most fashionable conspiracies of the past year: 5G antennas are used to spread the coronavirus, and Bill Gates is at the origin.

As with any working conspiracy theory, some things hold true:

Electromagnetic waves can be harmful and weaken human health.

The coronavirus is dangerous for human health.

Bill Gates, who made his fortune in Big Tech, has been devoted to philanthropy for many years and has advocated for vaccines.

Someone somewhere on the Internet has made a spurious link between 5G antennas and Covid-19; a narrative has been created: 5G damages human cells, so the coronavirus is more deadly for those same cells.

With the rhetoric that the powerful 'want to assert their power to raise even more money being taken as true by conspirators, Bill Gates's addition to this theory has been taken for granted, and the plot spread like wildfire; as a result, people ended up attacking 5G antennas, believing the installations were linked to the coronavirus.

Soon an AI application on social networks.

While the University of California's AI seems to be paying off, it is currently only available to researchers, and Professor Roychowdhury hopes that this invention will eventually have real positive effects on society.

Twitter signals when tweets may be fake news; the researchers hope that the social network will one day use their AI to clearly explain to users what false links gave rise to these plots.

Bill Gates on the conspiracy theories surrounding him

The multi-billionaire believes the pandemic will be ended before the end of 2021, and this is what Bill Gates said in an interview that made a splash in British magazine The Economist; he takes the opportunity to sweep away conspiracy theories that portray him as an evil genius.

Most of these deaths will not be caused by the virus itself but by economic hardship and the collapse of health infrastructure, and this is the grim prediction that Gates, widely regarded as a progress optimist, establishes in his conversation with the editor of the business magazine.

A cry in the desert

The billionaire and Microsoft co-founder is a relevant voice in the debate around Covid-19, the foundation fight against infectious diseases such as HIV, measles, and malaria.

The billionaire was not surprised by the pandemic; for years, the Microsoft boss has tried to warn the world it was only a matter of time before a global epidemic devastated life as we know it; he pleaded with the international community to prepare for it.

Devastating indirect effects

It is mainly the indirect effects that can cause death and destruction, he explains in his interview. Lockdowns limit access to care and medicine for other illnesses, which will increase the number of deaths from malaria and HIV.

Famine will start again because less land is worked, consequences: violence and migratory flows are expected. Decades of progress in poverty can be reversed.

Therefore, rich countries must fund vaccines for less prosperous countries, says the billionaire, not just out of charity, but for their benefit; as long as the virus remains dormant, anywhere, it can again reach pandemic proportions.

Conspiracy theories

Bill Gates estimates that 30 to 60% of the world's population will need an effective vaccine if the pandemic is stopped.

But since the start of the pandemic, Bill Gates has been the subject of conspiracy theories that link him to the origins of the coronavirus and to be in the pay of Big Pharma; a very persistent conspiracy theory suggests that Gates is considering using a Covid-19 vaccine to implant surveillance chips in billions of people.

The billionaire will not dwell on such misinformation in his interview with The Economist: "On a personal level, I do not care, but it affects the behavior of a section of the population and thus contributes to the delay in virus control. '

Why Bill Gates is the # 1 target of coronavirus conspirators?

Bill Gates is the main target of conspiracies and other fake news around the coronavirus that has been swarming on the Internet since the start of the crisis.

You may not have known it, but Bill Gates created the novel coronavirus; to enrich himself, even more, thanks to the vaccine, of course, unless, of course, it is for the simple pleasure of dominating the world.

These are the kinds of conspiracy theories that the name of Microsoft's founder has been linked to no less than 1.2 million times over the past three months on the Net.

In 2015, Bill Gates told a TED talk that his greatest fear for humankind was not nuclear war, but an uncontrolled pandemic, "If something kills more than 10 million people in the next decade, it will be a highly contagious virus.

It did not take more than five years later that anti-vaccines, conspirators, and far-right activists brandished the video as proof of guilt.

Other evidence against Bill Gates, the philanthropist would own the patent for a vaccine linked to the coronavirus through the English laboratory, the Pirbright Institute, which he partially funds, while the information is not wrong, the vaccine has nothing to do with the type of coronavirus that is currently hitting the world.

Either way, since the billionaire has pledged to finance the most promising vaccine projects with his fortune, this proves that he is looking for economic interest and, therefore, that he is guilty.

The limits of artificial intelligence to combat online disinformation

The past few years have been marked by the ever-increasing spread of disinformation, misinformation, poisoning, and other techniques for manipulating public opinion on social networks and online media.

The methods of computerized propaganda or computational propaganda are scrutinized and highlight the need to develop innovative tools to strengthen resilience in the face of disinformation.

Artificial intelligence via machine learning is, to date, one of the major tools used to fulfill this mission; however, it is necessary to integrate it into a more global framework for the fight against online disinformation.

The use of artificial intelligence to detect disinformation online.

Every day, more than a billion people on average use Facebook and are targets and vectors of spread; false content can target specific groups of individuals with similar characteristics or broader groups such as individuals with the right to vote, the expected results can range from manipulation of markets and share prices to social and political destabilization.

Machine learning, using behavioral analyzes and automatic language processing tools, can be used to detect disinformation, social media manipulation, cybercriminal attacks, the spread of conspiracy theories, and more.

A study by Rand Europe commissioned by the British Ministry of Defense has made it possible to model a system based on Machine learning; the latter makes it possible to detect, decode and understand the rhetoric used by malicious actors onlin.

The model identifies a linguistic and rhetorical signature in the data collected, this signature thus makes it possible to train the machine to detect the accounts of malicious actors.

In addition, the system scans the online network for malicious accounts and identifies connections and relationships between different accounts and groups: which account is connected to which account, which accounts have the same activity, which account is in which discussions or groups; 'online interest, Etc.

The system is thus able to model a network of trolls or robots within a social network.

Many cases of successful disinformation

The Brexit vote in June 2016 or the successful use of fake news: this was one of the first times that fake news had such an influence on an election, the Sun's edition that Queen Elisabeth II was pro-Brexit or Turkey's entry into the EU is all false information published in British media and shared on social media that influenced the vote.

The 2016 US presidential election is also often cited as an example; the involvement of Russian trolls is singled out: fake personas masquerading as real people on social media have been identified and attributed to Russians to crystallize internal American tensions during the election.

These trolls disseminated anti-racism messages along with messages about the threats of illegal immigration and Islam.

The aim is to illustrate the more controversial positions of the two parties and to instill the idea that the danger comes from the neighbor; the US government has reportedly identified at least 800 Twitter accounts controlled by Russian agents.

Finally, the latest example is the dissemination of false information related to the pandemic. Indeed, disinformation is a major feature of the COVID-19 crisis, the robots (or bot) on social networks are responsible for 45% to 60% of the content on the pandemic: the origin of the virus, treatments, vaccines, containment measures, and conspiracy theories.

These same robots have been twice as active since the onset of COVID-19 than in any other crisis or election; the private and public sectors have been severely damaged, not knowing how to combat this scourge.

Much erroneous information about the virus has circulated even within university teams to the point that a research project has been launched to identify and characterize fake news about the coronavirus.

This characterization focuses on their subject, the type of disinformation they contain, their modes, speeds, and distribution networks.

However, there is no mistaking the fight here: lies in politics or the public and economic life of a country are nothing new; only social networks allow it to spread on a large scale and reach an unprecedented number of readers, targeted or not.

The role of GAFAM in the fight against disinformation

GAFAMs are naturally at the forefront of the fight against online disinformation, many initiatives have been launched, and only these are still ineffective and have not avoided many controversies or even tragedies.

Indeed, by connecting to Twitter, if you view the most popular posts, most of them will be because robots will have "liked" and commented on these posts en masse, you will be able to identify this phenomenon by clicking on the accounts of the robots and by visualizing the very high frequency and speed of their posts.

For its part, Google has developed through its incubator Jigsaw, an artificial intelligence-based tool to combat hate speech and online trolls.

This tool is an API that developers use to detect toxic language automatically.

Mark Zuckerberg, meanwhile, facing the US Congress in April 2018, mentioned artificial intelligence more than 30 times, it will be the solution to the problem of digital disinformation, in particular, to deal with massive volumes.

Facebook, therefore, uses algorithms to identify and prioritize content according to a level of priority defined by them: from hate speech without a direct target to terrorist speech, violent and sexual images.

Despite all of these initiatives, a debate is open on the ineffectiveness of the passive posture of companies like Facebook.

Indeed, in 2019, the fact-checking site Snopes broke off its partnership with Facebook; the director of operations Vinny Green announced in an interview with the Poynter Institute "it does not seem like we are striving to make third-party fact-checking more practical for publishers - it seems like we are striving to make it easier for Facebook"; it seems that some companies have the sole aim of acting superficially against disinformation, with no real ambition to change things, but enough to protect their image.

According to Vinny Green, there is a need to develop a service based on artificial intelligence and machine learning, available through an API to the entire web, thus benefiting all people wishing to verify the information.

AI limits in the fight against disinformation

The first limit identified is structural: the solution put forward is precisely the cause of the problem, the deep fake is a perfect example of the informational threat enabled by artificial intelligence; this technique allows the creation and modification of audio-visual content of such a quality that it is very complex to identify the manipulation.

Images and videos, previously put forward as irrefutable evidence, can no longer be considered as such; moreover, cyber-criminals have already incorporated artificial intelligence into the paraphernalia of the tools they use.

Already in 2017, 62% of the speakers, experts in cybersecurity, of the Black Hat of Las Vegas already estimated that the cyber-criminals would use artificial intelligence to go on the offensive.

AI is often said to be a double-edged sword, on the one hand, it allows the emergence of increasingly sophisticated online informational threats and the lowering of the ramparts against malicious actors.

In particular, AI would be used to more precisely define the parameters of an informational attack: what, who and when to attack; on the other hand, AI presents many opportunities for tackling these same informational threats.

The second limitation is the ability of AI to make mistakes.

Artificial intelligence is now very much on the point of semantic detection; only certain aspects of language are still difficult for him to grasp; these are, for example, sarcasm, persuasion, or .

This is one of the reasons for the existence of false positives, major limitations of AI, designating a post as disinformation, abuse, or a troll when it is not, minimizes the spread of detection tools and their effectiveness.

The last limitation lies in human action before using the machine; the tools using Machine learning are configured by people who have their own cognitive biases; this raises the question of the objectivity of the machine's settings to determine what is false information and what is not.

Some platforms even use AI to identify content that is legal but defined by these same platforms as harmful: "inauthentic behavior" and "post insensitive" are targeted, beyond the question of objectivity, how we can accept that a platform defines the limit between the sensitive and the insensitive, the authentic and the authentic.

Towards a hybrid system - human and AI - more effective against disinformation

the problem has widened to a big data problem, and it would be inconceivable that the solution to the problem did not integrate artificial intelligence and machine learning.

However, the integration of human intelligence in the process for analyzing behavior and organizations is key; as specified in the Rand Europe study cited above, man must decipher the contexts, the organization of active groups but also the intellectual approach of an individual who allows himself to be convinced and adopts false information.

In addition, the informational threat is constantly evolving, and there is a need to adapt continuously; the approach must combine human knowledge, expertise from the social sciences to computer engineering and machine learning.

Some players, such as the WHO, are using machine learning to target their communication strategy better.

This practice called social listening involves collecting more than 1.5 million social media posts each week; a machine learning algorithm analyzes the collected data to classify information: cause, disease, interventions, and treatments, by identifying popular topics, WHO wants to deploy more targeted communication and thus show right from wrong to those most interested.

Another approach would detect disinformation through the path taken by the information; researchers from the Swiss Federal Institute of Technology in Lausanne have thus set up a User Credit Record, the latter is assigned to each account that propagates, consults, shares information on social networks depending on whether it is true or not.

Rather than studying the content of each piece of information, our solution looks at the credulity history of its propagators, tell me where this news went, I will tell you if it is serious or misleading: this is kind of the idea on which our approach is based.

A posture issue to be adopted concerning the informational threat.

The posture of the web giants in particular towards disinformation must be corrected in order to be more proactive, and it is necessary to stop reacting and correcting a posteriori but attempting to detect threats before their spread to limit their effects.

The first conclusive results have just recently emerged, researchers at the University of Sheffield have developed an AI system that makes it easier to detect a user who publishes fake news before it is massively shared.

State action, for its part, must be organized around the fight against disinformation as recommended by the European Commission and the report (2019) of the "Regulation of social networks - Facebook experiment" mission; this would include the creation of common databases to improve tools for combating disinformation and the sharing of research making it possible to detect repetitive rhetorical patterns on a large scale.

The public must be aware of the methods and techniques of disinformation and the detection of rhetorical patterns that play on their emotions; this awareness could, in particular, be achieved through public service announcements.

These would make it possible to convey awareness messages pushing for the adaptation of attitudes and behaviors about informational threats, and this in particular upstream of electoral periods.

An experiment carried out made it possible to conclude that messages of this type were considered as positive by the majority of the participants, in particular, those about foreign interference during an election period and only if these messages come from legitimate sources of authority.

The fight against disinformation will therefore go through a model combining artificial intelligence and human action, but also and above all through alignment around a common strategy between governments, private information dissemination platforms, and the public, two prerequisites are inevitable: awareness around a pooled action and awareness of the general public to informational threats.

CHAPTER 6:
METAVERSE

Metaverse

Currently, Metaverse buzzword, but many ignore that it is changing the gaming industry, the social industry, even the simple way of life; this is why it has become the most recent macro lens of most of the world's tech giants, it is also the driving force behind Facebook's purchase of Oculus VR.

The term metaverse comes from the two words, Meta and universe; it comes from the English word metaverse, which refers to various virtual experiences, environments, and assets.

It also means an experience in a three-dimensional virtual environment, where it is possible to evolve through an avatar or a hologram; this alternative reality makes it possible to discuss with other people and learn, work or even play.

The metaverse reality (AR) and virtual reality (VR) create a collective universe; thanks to these cutting-edge techniques, the metaverse rules of verbal and non-verbal communication are similar to reality: gestures, facial expressions, tone of voice.

Typically, it is used to describe the concept of a future Internet iteration, made up of persistent, shared, and 3D virtual spaces linked in a perceived virtual universe; in 1982, you could not imagine what the Internet would be like in 2020.

Metaverse characteristics

It is believed that anyone will be able to be a part of the metaverse in a specific event or activity together; it will provide a personal feeling of "presence" to each user; it will also be a fully functioning economy, the metaverse an experience that encompasses both digital and physical worlds.

In addition, this internet revolution will allow unprecedented interoperability of data, content, and digital assets; some will be independent individuals, others may be informally organized groups or commercial enterprises.

The most recent concept should not be Metacosm; it is not true; in addition to being corroborated by on-chain data, the activity of metacosm-related communities at home and abroad and daily communication with their peers are Also noticeable.

First of all, that is for sure, Metaverse the start. It is on this basis that, although many of the greats have posted their reviews on Metaverse 's finding and definition of, there is never Had a consistent response.

Instead, most readers blurred their concept; although Metaverse clear in what form the opening and closing will take place, some predictable features have emerged.

Predictable characteristics

A superior social system to the current Internet

Web2.0, to some extent, the social system has eliminated geo-restrictions, but it is still much less than the real world in terms of experience and immersion and based on metaverse's world-building, We will bring a social experience that is no different or better than the real world; besides being silicon-based life friends, apart from aliens society, maybe we could also AI NPC Become friends.

A more independent and open economic system

Compared to the real world, Metaverse pendent economic system, more democratic and more open; at that time, all eco - users will work together as a community of destiny to maintain this vast system, bad economic decisions, due to dictatorship or to humanity, can be avoided to some extent.

A more authentic and immersive Internet identity

Web2.0 Games or social platforms are currently only "Play" Phase; at best, it is an accessory to real life, and Metaverse to the real world, what it will give us will be "Experience," in Metaverse is no essential difference with staying in the real world, In the future people will have the right to decide the real world and

Metaverse and, Maybe for someone who wants to live Metaverse, the world only serves to complement the functioning of the body.

The metaverse of inspiration in the cultural world

Books, films, video games, the virtual world inspires in multiple cultural sectors. When it comes to cinema, of course, we think of the dystopian universe of the Matrix or, more recently, the Steven Spielberg film Ready Player One.

Eight elements that make up a meta-universe product, according to Roblox

According to Roblox, eight main elements make up a true meta-universe product:

Identity: You have a VID, whether or not it is linked to a real identity.

Immersion: You will be immersed in the meta-universe experience.

Diversification: The Meta universe provides various and rich content, including gameplay, props, and art materials

An economic system: Like any large-scale complex game, the metaverse have its own economic system.

One Contact: You have contacts in the metaverse that can socialize whether you know them or not.

Low latency: Everything in the meta-universe runs synchronously, without asynchrony or delay.

Anytime Accessibility: You can use any device to sign in and dive into Metaverse anywhere.

A Civilization: The meta-universe should be a virtual civilization.

Relationship with blockchain

Metaverse opportunities created and developed in recent years include VR Improved infrastructure popularity of distributed commerce, online habit formation, demand for virtual goods and services, and the epidemic pushing and Blockchain is Metaverse Important core technology for landing, Especially NFT an important contribution to clarifying ownership and increasing authenticity, NFT The game can be seen as a relationship between the present and the Metaverse the most appropriate direction.

DeWeb2 Perception in the game

From a gaming perspective, this is because the virtual space built by the game is probably the fastest at Metaverse Entry, game visualization, Interesting, Enabling people to explore unknown virtual worlds while gaining spiritual pleasure.

Although games are just culture, entertainment, media is one of the big areas of the industry, but we think it is related Metaverse lost closely related because it is Metaverse economy in a whole new universe, culture, art, community, Microcosm of governance, Etc.

Sandbox Games

In many game types, the Sandbox game is currently the closest morphologically to Metaverse, the maps are usually larger, with NPC Or the environment is very interactive, lots of content.

With a high degree of freedom, can be explored more freely, create and modify game content, non-linear games often also have linear modes to choose from, but in general the player is not required to complete a task or set goals.

Refine the concepts, and the sandbox game has a high degree of freedom and openness features.

If added VR \ AR Support equipment, Etc., superimpose a good degree of near-truth, this will be essential for Metaverse players immersion.

What the Metaverse

Metaverse he word metaverse is used incorrectly, it is sometimes seen as a virtual world, which is not correct; virtual worlds and games with AI-driven characters have been around for decades, as have those populated by real humans in real-time, this is not a meta-universe; this is just a synthetic and fictional universe designed for one purpose, the metaverse is a virtual space nor a virtual reality.

Also, the metaverse game, it is true that it has game-like object-ives, it includes games and involves gamification, but it is not in itself a game; nor is it geared around specific goals, finally, the metaverse other YouTube or Facebook-like platform in which countless people can create, share and monetize content.

How important is the metaverse

Potential to produce trillions of value, is the metaverse the gate-way to most digital experiences? It is a key part of all physical ex-periences and the next great platform for work.

And if the metaverse is a functional successor to the web, there will likely be even more economic benefits; it should produce the same variety of opportunities we have seen with the web; new companies, products, and services will emerge to handle every-thing from payment processing and identity verification, hiring, ad serving and content creation.

More broadly, the metaverse potential to change the way we al-locate and monetize modern resources; real estate has increased and decreased, under the metaverse workers who choose to live outside cities will be able to participate in the high-value econ-omy through virtual work.

Are we currently close to a real metaverse?

Still, a few obstacles to a true metaverse; hardware limitations are one of them; indeed, today, global networking and comput-ing capabilities are not yet able to support a persistent digital world.

The energy consumption of such an enterprise would create problems for both national electricity grids and the environment; technological limitations aside, there is another big challenge, interoperability.

Currently, even so-called metaverse precursors such as Fortnite do not allow players to recreate their user-generated content on other platforms; to enable true interoperability between platforms, companies that own these platforms must relinquish some control over the content and user experience of their player bases; this process is already underway.

Sony, a notorious resistance to cross-platform gaming, recently moved to allow PlayStation users to interact with gamers on other consoles more frequently.

Although its future users may know it as the Internet, the metaverse table, it will happen incrementally, as cultural changes and technological upgrades give internet users the ability to move more and more freely and easily to create and share bespoke content on the web.

Just as there has been no formal change between Web 1.0 to Web 2.0, the metaverse ally occurs.

While "Fortnite" and "Roblox" are often described as precursors to the metaverse important precursor to the metaverse internet itself.

But if the Internet was a video tour of the apartment, giving a brief overview of each room in a defined sequence, the metaverse the apartment itself; we may not live there yet, but we have already signed the lease.

With the creation of limited-time virtual exhibition space alongside the physical Gucci Garden event, the luxury brand, which had decided to market its products in virtual format for the occasion, achieved the feat of selling a more expensive virtual bag than its physical version.

The connection is easy between the metaverse, which provides access to unique digital title deeds.

The metaverse offers multiple opportunities for brands; on the other hand, it is important to distinguish between the consumer and the avatar they have created for themselves.

Indeed, users imagine a character in their likeness while modifying the details of their choices; marketing actions are therefore aimed at fictitious representations, and it becomes difficult to envision personae as close as possible to the reality of end consumers.

Can the metaverse the rules of our society?

Besides the world of video games, the metaverse is deeply embedded in society; it seems that the various confinements have accelerated the digitization process in everyday life and companies.

In 2020, Facebook launched Horizon, a virtual reality, a multiplayer social network that works with the Oculus VR headset.

After entertainment, the Facebook group is now tackling the world of work with the Oculus Horizon Workrooms project, which proposes to use a metaverse to allow employees to meet virtually in a meeting room, as shown in the video below.

To go even further, Mark Zuckerberg now employs 10,000 people to work on virtual reality and augmented reality.

In an interview with the Verge, the entrepreneur said he sees the metaverse internet embodied, where instead of just watching the content, you are in it, so the race to conquer the metaverse end Facebook is careful to get there first.

The metaverse at the ground for tech giants

Now that he has got the mobile world under his thumb, Mark Zuckerberg has his eyes set on a new realm: the metaverse future of Facebook as a company, assured the manager to his share-holders on the occasion of the last presentation of Facebook's results; but what is the metaverse?

It is a virtual universe which will seem familiar to the few who have read Neal Stephenson's book, Snow Crash, published in 1992 and to those who, more numerous, have seen Steven Spielberg's film, Ready Player One.

It is, according to the American VC, Matthew Ball, author of numerous articles on the subject, a virtual, live, persistent and open environment; so that each user can transport their avatar and their belongings from one part of the metaverse, no matter who manages that part.

We necessarily think of Second Life, this virtual universe that buzzed in the early 2000s, affecting up to 30 million users, before falling back into oblivion, swept away in particular by the revolution.

The big difference between the metaverse ebook wants to set up and that of Second Life is the addressable market, it is no longer the prerogative of a few geeks, as numerous as they were in the days of Second Life.

Today, the vast majority of the population can navigate these worlds, the coronavirus has been there and, with it, numerous confinement and social distancing measures that have pushed a whole section of the population to go digital; for several months, the physical world was reduced to an area of 1km.

The other difference is the evolution of technology, no connected glasses like Snapchat Spectacles or Facebook Glasses in the Second Life era, or even virtual reality headsets like Facebook's Oculus or Microsoft's Hololens.

Uses are still in their infancy, and manufacturers are still a long way from designing devices that are both easy to wear and technologically advanced, but democratization is underway, and with it, that of the metaverse will only have meaning if you can get there via a device that allows you to navigate it spatially, which is not possible with a computer mouse, Epic Games have recently acquired the platform.

Sketchfab, which contains 4 million 3D assets that can be sold, bought, or edited, should allow the owner of Fortnite to get closer to an open and interconnected metaverse.

Sketchfab allows everyone to get their hands on avatars or environments, such as the 3D version of the planet Mars, which will make it possible to offer experiences in the metaverse giant to the architect of the metaverse only one step, seems to believe its new shareholder, Epic Games had already begun its transformation into full containment, hosting a concert by rapper Travis Scott who brought together no less than 12 million users in April 2020.

The American, which brings together more than 350 million players on Fortnite, will have to nevertheless deal with top competitors like Roblox or Minecraft, who also want their share of the metaverse brings together forty million players every day and has been valued at $ 50 billion since its IPO in April 2021, Roblox has just announced a partnership with the Vans brand, resulting in the creation of an animated universe called Vans World, in which fans of the brand can go skating, wearing their favorite Vans, in a virtual version of their favorite skatepark.

No more Roblox than Epic or Minecraft is, for the moment, able to transpose their users in the metaverse of being able to offer persistent environments, but they are approaching it very slowly.

It is also a whole economy that has been set up in Roblox's Vans World, with some items that will be free but most of which will be accessible via the local virtual currency, the Robux.

The metaverse gaming, the realm of the freemium model is a kingdom where you will have to pay to stand out like what is already done in Fortnite, where it is a whole economy of the skin that has developed.

Epic, the gaming giant, had communicated on the sales of skins made last November during a partnership with the NFL, with a total of 3.3 million skins sold for $ 15 each, it made nearly $ 50 million in revenue in just two months.

This is just the beginning as more and more brands are investing in these up and coming metaverse, which also announced last July a partnership with Roblox, allowing users of the gaming platform to dress their avatar in the brand's clothes.

The metaverse is confined to entertainment at least; that is what Facebook hopes for with the launch of its virtual meeting rooms, the Workrooms, which can be accessed via an Oculus Quest 2 headset.

From a meeting Zoom, where static cameras limit interactions, to a Workroom meeting, where interactivity would be stronger, there is only one step that many want to take, assured Andrew Bosworth, vice-president of Facebook Reality Labs, on the occasion of the beta presentation.

Fans of remote work will decide, but this first attempt by the Facebook laboratory remains a technological feat when we know that an environment like Workroom must, on its own, allow the capture of participants' hand movements, the flows of their computers, as well as the video and audio that concerns them.

This is only the first step towards a more successful experience, Facebook wants to go further by offering interactions with virtual objects making it possible to explain things more easily.

The metaverse is a reality, but many are already claiming its authorship; it must be said that, for gaming giants like Epic Games, Roblox, and Minecraft, it has become a matter of sovereignty; a way out to the Internet as we know it today, where walled gardens like Facebook, Google and Amazon are making more acquisitions to strengthen the thickness of their walls and where an Apple makes it rain and shine.

In the application world, thanks to IOS, by switching to the metaverse could free themselves from Apple, for example, by controlling everything themselves, where on mobile, they must deal with the rules of the firm at apple and its commissions of 15 to 30%, we can also see in the lawsuit that currently opposes Epic Games to Apple the first battle of a long-term war and should, sooner or later, move to the metaverse.

Against big tech

The boss of Epic has also pleaded that the outcome of this trial would be crucial for the creation of the metaverse will be very complicated for Epic and the creators to exist in a future where Apple takes a commission of 30%, he assured the judges, the boss of Epic won the first battle, but he knows that the road is long.

Epic has made openness and interoperability one of its hobby-horses, the challenge is not to own the metaverse provide tools that allow everyone to create their own one.e

Meantime, everyone is working on their weapons, gaming players have mastered the language that will make the meta-verse have 10 years of experience in social gaming, the GAFA have, for them, almost unlimited resources and a certain mas-tery of the hardware, the metaverse opportunity for Marc Zuckerberg to justify the $ 2 billion spent on Oculus technology in 2014.

Without really having a return on investment for the moment; for Apple and Google, it is necessary to transpose their pa-tents and the technical knowledge accumulated via their OS and smartphone to new devices: connected glasses, voice assistants, the fight between gaming giants and GAFA, therefore, turns to the eternal hardware duality versus software.

It is difficult to know, at this stage, which of the site managers, the players in gaming, or the holders of the access doors, will have the most power.

Why build the metaverse?

The Internet has created new markets and new opportunities, so too is the metaverse ducts and services will emerge, giving birth to companies well-positioned to capitalize on the needs of the Metaverse people who use it; this change may mean that other incumbents may become obsolete if they do not get behind the wheel from the start.

The metaverse will surpass anything we have seen, and the metaverse can create an immersive experience in a whole new virtual space.

There will certainly be ads throughout the Metaverse ends can go beyond that and help build the Metaverse almost all the top internet companies' rank among the most valuable public companies in the world;

Before the metaverse, it will need a competing infrastructure, and then it will need defined standards and protocols to work; finally, it should be filled with content.

Creating the metaverse, the capacities of singular people requires resources beyond our reach, the metaverse to be built by a set of organizations and IT professionals.

The players

Who will build the metaverse likely be a combination of businesses and individuals that will help creating it, the Metaverse in its infancy, but some pioneers having already made it clear their intention to build it.

Epic games

If there is currently one leader rising to the forefront of this technological race, it is Epic Games, and as the maker of Fortnite, Epic Games already operates one of the platforms closest to what the Metaverse come, Fortnite started as a game that evolved into a social square with its economy where users can create and monetize their content.

The metaverse requires an unprecedented level of interoperability to be functional; Fortnite has already demonstrated its ability to bring together competitors in cooperative alliances; this game develops a shared virtual space where brands and players can interact in a way similar to how the metaverse work.

The systems and platforms operated by Microsoft have hundreds of millions of users, coupled with their technical background and infrastructure, the metaverse apple operates the most valuable computing platform and the largest game store, he has demonstrated his willingness to invest in the metaverse of his investments; the company has invested money in augmented reality devices that can affect the way we connect with the metaverse.

If we are to have augmented reality that adds virtual enhancements to physical reality, we will need a 3D digital map of the real world.

Google is the leader in indexing the digital world and conquering the intuitive ad placement market, and Google runs Android, the most widely used operating system; it also has a sprawling investment portfolio, and the metaverse is probably the one thing that can unite all of Google's assets.

Advantages and disadvantages

Users will benefit from the technological race in which these companies are engaged; their drive to shape the metaverse translates into new technology, better gameplay, and new experiences.

The metaverse needs games that all of their friends can play for users, regardless of what hardware or platforms they use; Garena strategically designed Free Fire to take up little disk space and maximize their user base.

The metaverse how users further customize and create, companies like Digitalax are using NFTs as an efficient distribution channel and building a digital supply chain; this company is building the basic infrastructure for the Metaverse initiatives in fashion and games.

Another essential aspect of social gaming is the cross-play between systems such as Epic Game's offering of its suite of online services, such an ability for games to talk to each other will be part of the metaverse will require contestants to give up their ideas.

The downside to these metaverse-building tech giants is the potential to create monopolies that can crush the competition and thwart creativity; suppose a privileged few invest heavily in creating the metaverse framework, in this case, they will surely expect to capitalize on this investment by pushing back external competition; the result can be a lack of variety in the gaming industry and a stagnant market.

It is hard to say when so much of what we know about the Metaverse relative, it is a huge business, and we need tech giants to take the reins because only they have enough resources to bring the Metaverse as to how this will turn out, only time will tell.

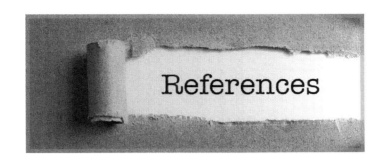

CHPATER 7:
REFERENCES

References

https://www.oracle.com/fr/artificial-intelligence/deep-learning-machine-learning-intelligence-artificielle.html

https://www.coe.int/fr/web/artificial-intelligence/what-is-ai

https://www.ionos.fr/digitalguide/web-marketing/vendre-sur-internet/quest-ce-que-lintelligence-artificielle/

https://www.20minutes.fr/high-tech/2982935-20210301-pourquoi-intelligence-artificielle-demain-beaucoup-plus-rapide-plus-ecologique

https://www.science-et-vie.com/technos-et-futur/labos-10-defis-pour-l-avenir-54455

https://www.businessinsider.fr/on-vous-explique-comment-elon-musk-pense-mettre-des-puces-dans-le-cerveau-des-gens-163937

https://parlonssciences.ca/ressources-pedagogiques/documents-dinformation/introduction-a-lapprentissage-machine

https://www.forcepoint.com/fr/cyber-edu/machine-learning

https://www.lebigdata.fr/machine-learning-et-big-data

https://substance.etsmtl.ca/differences-intelligence-artificielle-apprentissage-machine-apprentissage-profond

https://www.stemmer-imaging.com/fr-ch/conseil-techniqu/apprentissage-automatique-et-apprentissage-profond/

https://www.ionos.fr/digitalguide/web-marketing/analyse-web/quest-ce-que-lapprentissage-automatique/

https://www.lemagit.fr/conseil/Machine-Learning-les-9-types-dalgorithmes-les-plus-pertinents-en-entreprise

https://morethandigital.info/fr/apprentissage-automatique-les-bases-et-la-definition-sont-expliquees-pour-les-debutants-et-les-managers/

https://www.spiria.com/fr/blogue/intelligence-artificielle/3-etapes-essentielles-apprentissage-automatique-machine-learning/

https://datascience.eu/fr/apprentissage-automatique/top-6-des-techniques-dapprentissage-machine/

https://www.processmaker.com/fr/blog/machine-learning-past-present-future/

https://www.cisin.com/coffee-break/fr/enterprise/highlights-the-advantages-and-disadvantages-of-machine-learning.html

https://www.futura-sciences.com/tech/definitions/technologie-realite-virtuelle-598/

https://filmora.wondershare.fr/virtual-reality/pros-cons-virtual-virtual.html?gclid=EAIaIQobChMIwtry-ePu8gIVsmDm-Ch09YwMwEAAYAiAAEgIYB_D_BwE

https://www.vteducation.org/fr/articles/realite-virtuelle/10-outils-de-creation-de-realite-virtuelle

https://www.sanofi.fr/fr/labsante/Quelles-sont-les-applications-de-la-realite-virtuelle-en-sante

https://www.dynamique-mag.com/article/gerer-stress-periodes-fortes-activites.4043

https://www.lesechos.fr/idees-debats/sciences-prospective/jusquou-peut-aller-la-realite-virtuelle-1155053

https://www.augmented-reality.fr/cest-quoi-la-realite-augmentee/

https://www.3demotion.net/la-realite-augmentee/

https://ohrizon.com/technologies-realite-augmentee/

https://www.sanofi.fr/fr/labsante/Focus-sur-les-benefices-de-la-realite-virtuelle-et-augmentee-dans-la-smart-industry

https://www.place-communication.com/la-realite-augmentee-defis-et-limites/

https://realitevirtuelleetaugmentee.wordpress.com/avantages-et-inconvenients-2/

https://www.forbes.fr/technologie/les-dangers-de-la-realite-virtuelle-augmentee-ou-etendue/

https://theconversation.com/theories-du-complot-de-quoi-ne-parle-t-on-pas-162485

https://www.franceculture.fr/emissions/le-tour-du-monde-des-idees/le-tour-du-monde-des-idees-du-mercredi-17-mars-2021

https://www.huffingtonpost.fr/entry/comment-faire-face-aux-theories-du-complot-a-lheure-du-covid-19-blog_fr_5fbf-c936c5b66bb88c64f8c8

https://www.quebecscience.qc.ca/sante/covid-19-these-acci-dent-laboratoire/

https://www.univ-rennes1.fr/actualites/crise-sanitaire-et-the-ories-du-complot

https://www.20minutes.fr/arts-stars/cul-ture/3033475-20210506-comment-ia-train-rendre-tous-para-noiaques

https://trustmyscience.com/comment-theories-complot-emer-gent-et-seffrondrent/

https://www.tomsguide.fr/cette-intelligence-artificielle-differ-encie-les-theories-du-complot-et-les-veritables-conspirations/

https://lactualite.com/societe/a-quoi-ressemblerait-une-ortog-rafe-rationele/

https://www.ouest-france.fr/leditiondusoir/2021-09-06/une-theorie-du-complot-affirme-quinternet-est-mort-depuis-2016-73427393-4453-4b08-b85e-be4a6712844f

https://fr.businessam.be/simple-theorie-du-complot-ou-verit-able-conspiration-cette-ia-permet-de-trancher/

https://fr.businessam.be/pourquoi-bill-gates-est-la-cible-n1-des-complotistes-du-coronavirus/

https://www.ege.fr/infoguerre/les-limites-de-lintelligence-artificielle-pour-combattre-la-desinformation-en-ligne

https://ichi.pro/fr/que-pouvons-nous-attendre-d-un-metaverse-construit-par-les-plus-grandes-plateformes-de-jeu-18699863349019

https://netfreeman.com/2021/08/20210824204323824y.html

https://www.realite-virtuelle.com/le-metaverse-tout-savoir/

https://www.blogdumoderateur.com/metaverse-univers-virtuel-attire-geants-tech/

https://www.journaldunet.com/media/publishers/1505369-le-metaverse-nouveau-terrain-de-bataille-des-geants-de-la-tech/

ABOUT THE AUTHOR

Lhachmi Taifouri

LHACHMI TAIFOURI is a product of the '60s and father of three children; he was born in Southeast of Morocco in a Berber community, graduated in the technical field in the early '80s, and got a business administration Ph.D. with a high degree.

In a former life, he has been working for Multinational corporations in the oil and gas field for over 30 years; he had occupied many positions in logistics, aviation, and others.

As an entrepreneur and self-employed in the consulting field and as a member of the world order of international experts based in Geneva, Switzerland, he is extremely fond of analysis and studies in sociology sciences and geostrategic studies.

His work across many disciplines broadly addresses the narratives of human experience.

His educational and experiences background has given him bases from which to approach many topics and provided many opportunities to him, especially defending and supporting human rights everywhere.

When he is not working or writing, LHACHMI TAIFOURI envoys listening to music, reading, and trying new things; his other talents include cooking and dropping and spilling things around.

Drop him a line anytime, whether it is about a comment or feedback or to say Hi.

BOOKS BY THIS AUTHOR

Upside Wiser

Nowadays, we live in worlds that change constantly and quickly. We see here and there many issues related to human beings and their interaction with their environment; the last decades will have been those of a considerable transformation of life and work, costumes and mentalities, the acceleration of knowledge, and access to information.

Our modern world shapes our behaviors and gives us an illusion of autonomy in doing things and understanding all kinds of issues.

The advancement in the Internet of things, virtual reality, and Artificial intelligence do not let us think outside the box; we are immerging in this sophisticated world without our contentment.

UPSIDE WISER provides you with an amazing scale of information and facts that will grab your attention and put another brick to your big knowledge building.
Moreover, it takes you to an incredible journey that, step by step, helps you understand deeply many issues that we face in our everyday life and highlight things that may be skipped by many of us due to a lack of time and availability.

Beliefs'spirit

Sometimes a person programs himself through the restrictive beliefs and societal classifications that he imbibes through the people around him so that internal conversations begin here that are not positive but rather orders and mockery of the self.

Beliefs may sometimes be blunt assumptions or perceptions of the self, formed either from external thoughts or personal experiences of previous situations, which control the self, restricting our thoughts to become an obstacle to achieving future goals.

You may face some unexpected and traumatic situations due to negative thoughts and random decisions that are not sufficiently studied, and eventually, you find yourself reaching the unexpected result simply because you planted the seeds of society and others within you and got what people want and not what you want.

Our emotions and behavior have their roots in beliefs, they shape our life, and our experiences are expressed and interpreted according to them.

We could put beliefs between good and evil, beauty and ugliness, acceptable and unacceptable, moral and immoral, pain and gentleness.

The majority of our beliefs are satisfactory; however, the few unsatisfactory create a feeling of emotional instability; what affects us is freezing a belief because this goes against the life which is in perpetual motion.

BELIEFS SPIRIT comes to take you on a fascinating journey through events such as spirit, religion, dogmas and highlights many behaviors that could come from someone's beliefs and lead to extremism; radicalism terrorism acts as the extreme consequences.

BELIEFS SPIRIT ultimate goal is not to get rid of our beliefs but rather to find our life balance within them.

BELIEFS SPIRIT did not pretend to master that field's topics but give you in-depth information about the origins of beliefs and unusual consequences of some kind of them; it also tries to explain some unexpected ways taken by radicalizes extremists, and terrorists.

People Vs. People

We see and hear everywhere, and among us, disabled people that became overtime trivial and no one pays attention to, because they are part of our normal life; so describing the inequalities that affect people with disabilities assumes that there is a clear distinction between people with disabilities and those without; however, the distinction between them is more complex than age, sex or migratory origin, it is based on criteria relating to the condition of persons which include a greater degree of subjectivity.

Over one billion people, or about 15% of the world's population, have some form of disability; the number of disabled people is on the rise, this is due, among other things, to demographic trends and the increasing prevalence of chronic diseases.

Almost everyone is likely to experience some form of disability, temporary or permanently, at some point in their life; people with disabilities are particularly vulnerable and more affected by today's issues like the COVID-19 pandemic.

There is much kind of disabilities today than before, from mental ones to physical ones, to today chronically disease, to aging and, had different origins and different consequences, and their issues depends on where they are located, developed countries or poor ones, and where they are born, poor families or rich ones.

Fortunately, everything is not dark. There are some stories of the most famous people on the international level that are succeeded in overcoming their disabilities and becoming masters in their field, surpassing even normal people.

The accessibility to new technologies for the disabled, in this digital age, is a valuable technical aid; each user must be able to perceive, understand, navigate, and interact easily; the goal is to make everyone evolve at the same pace, without anyone being left out; these amounts to saying that the new technologies alleviate the difficulties of people with physical or mental disabilities.

From this perspective, assistive technology for the disabled must respond to a real challenge, circumventing different obstacles faced by disabled people; this is how they can enjoy the same privileges, whether in a personal or professional setting.

PEOPLE vs. PEOPLE do not pretend to master any related topics but tried to give the readers a broad picture of todays' disabilities facts, figure out its future, and highlight all kinds of issues they face off in their day-to-day lives.

Information Circle

Information is the new thing added to a person's intellectual, cognitive, or scientific inventory, and a person can obtain information from various sources.

Some people obtain information from books; others obtain it from hearing and learning, and others from experience and scientific evidence.

The importance of information is undoubtedly great for all people of all cultures and disciplines of knowledge.

All people need information, whether a simple farmer cultivates his land to a scientist who invents advanced tools that serve people.

Information is a source of creativity and innovation in the life, as many scientists and innovators are always keen to collect information in all fields that expand their perceptions and horizons of thinking and produce the juice of their brains reflected in innovations that serve humanity.

With the development of the Internet, AI, VR, and IoT, information became more and more crucial, especially with social media, where misinformation and manipulation expanded to the point that we were no longer able to differentiate the true from the false.

Overall, we witness gradual and generalized networking of society linked to the emergence of a new informational development mode.

The digital society creates addictions to permanent connection, to virtual universes, to make communications and exchanges summary due to technical mediation, to offer unreliable content, if not dangerous for certain people such as children, and jeopardize copyright.

It is also perceived as weakening individual freedoms and seems to sound the death knell for private life as the border between private life and public life is permeable, and the possibilities for remote surveillance are increasing.

That is why INFORMATION CIRCLE brings you all information aspects and its environments; it will take you on an amazing journey inside this vast universe, through many stations that tried to explain and highlight topics that interfere with the correct and true information.

INFORMATION CIRCLE tried to make it easier for you to understand all topics related to misinformation and its impact on the era in which we live that become rippled with much information, including the right and the wrong; in order to avoid mistakes and failure in life, as information is always the key to success.

To Be

We all know that our health as humankind and our way of living is important because they make it easier for us to achieve our goals in life; for this reason, we need to know what to do to stay healthy and happy.

Furthermore, to live happily, long, and in good health do not require any fame and money, which some may consider as the miracle recipe ingredients.

Therefore, being happy and in good health is neither easy nor a given for the whole life, so our health and our mood may not always be perfect, but we expect us to do what we could to have the best possible; we need both a healthy body and mind.

That is why TO BE comes to introduce you to all the topics related to the human universe of health and happiness and high-lights all the aspects of health issues and barriers that stop us from living happy from childhood to the elderly and retired.

You do not need to resolve to improve your life, as there are many simple changes you can make at any time; being happy and healthy requires just a little desire and motivation.

Community, friends, and family play an important role in our life and have a huge impact on us. Hence, people closest to their family, friends, or community are happier and healthier.

Having closed relationships can also protect us from the vagaries of aging, from pain but also memory loss.

As said by a wiser, let us seek to extend the present life as much as possible, observe all the laws of health and balancing work, study, rest, and entertainment properly and prepare ourselves for a better life. In the end, we have to teach these principles to the next generation.

Values'roots

As shown by Maslow in his well-known pyramid needs, humans have different needs levels, and there are first necessities like food, water, air, a roof, clothes without which the survival of the organism is not possible; once these needs are met, man moves to meet higher needs such as social needs, security needs or the need for self-improvement.

Values are among them and are perceptions that will lead to preferential behavior; they are considered as criteria for choosing from among the behavioral alternatives available to the individual in a situation.

Therefore, the individual embracing certain values means expecting him to engage in behavioral activities consistent with those values.

The influence of family, society, and culture makes each person unique; the values developed to define each person's priorities and lifestyle determines the individual's growth, family, society, nation, and humanity.

The values of judgments acquired from social conditions that the individual imbibes and governs, and define areas of his thinking, determine his behavior, and influence his learning, as he sees that social values mean the characteristics that people prefer or desire in a particular culture, and take the characteristic of generality for all individuals as they become behavior guides or are considered his goals.

Therefore, each person does not follow the same path; the path taken will depend on the inherent values of the person, and these inherent valuesare acquired under its nature, its experiences; we, therefore, shape them through our lives and have many roots; it could be religion, or our mind, or society.

VALUES' ROOTS comes to take you on a new journey through the large values circle and highlight them based on our everyday life; as we know, each individual can have different values; it could be happiness, courage, and dedication.

A wide range of factors can influence a person's values; however, it is also possible for a person to change their values over time.

VALUES' ROOTS do not pretend to master any related topics but tried to give the readers a broad picture of how it was built and shaped through time and space.

Vision Of The Next

We are all concerned about the future, in everyday life, we move toward our destiny, and we try to plan for tomorrow to get a better life for ourselves and our children; but we all know that the future could not ever be predicted; we just put hypothesis and expectations and hope we will be right or near right and encounter them.

No one can predict what mutations will occur and what kind of humans might result from them tomorrow.

We practically all have the same desires, aspirations, and desires worldwide, and yet conflicts, wars, genocides, famines, repressions, rapes, murders, assassinations, and all gratuitous violence is repeated every day within humanity.

To foresee the future, you have to know the past and the present; the man had already benefited from major technological and social advances a few decades ago; in particular of the industrial revolution, which engendered many changes in the way of working and of thinking as well as changes of social orders, and the arrival of the internet which upset the established order by accelerating the exchanges of information between people.

Technological advances in synthetic biology and genetic engineering make the militarization of pathogens easier and less expensive.; climate change will have devastating consequences, and we have nowhere to go; the collapse of the global ecosystem could halt the Earth's ability to support a growing human population; scarcity of water on the planet that will be a source of social and economic tensions which could one day become extremely serious.

We are wasting the Earth's riches on futile and stupid mass consumption; the planet's ecological balances are fundamentally weakened by industrial pollution, and there are other risks to humanity that scientists have not even imagined yet.

The legitimate question that we could put on ourselves is the main challenges facing humanity tomorrow?

VISION OF THE NEXT aims to bring you yesterday and today's big picture and try to give you some hypothesis of tomorrow's future.

We could take some actions today and such as avoiding the excesses of science that have largely become techno science, increasingly close to the market; reducing pollution and fighting against global climate change; protecting biodiversity and stemming the depletion of resources; curbing soil erosion and desertification; finding the means to feed billions human beings; intelligent machines could wipe out humans if left unchecked.

Two opposing dynamics will probably play a determining role on the planet; on the one hand, the interests of large, globalized firms, driven by financial concerns, which use techno science exclusively for profit; on the other hand, an aspiration for ethics, responsibility, and more equitable development that considers environmental constraints that are no doubt vital for the future of humanity.

VISION OF THE NEXT does not pretend to master any related topics but tried to give the readers a broad picture of today's facts and how they could impact humanity's future.

Today's Monopolies

We see and hear here and there our humankind manipulated and become subject to speculation, especially our health, our mind, and our wellbeing; that manipulation comes from small groups that consider themselves smart and genius; those groups have many names such as monopolies, oligopolies, cartels, GAFAM, BATX, BIG PHARMA, to name few.

These issues have always existed since the beginning, but today it takes a huge part of our lives, if not to say our whole lives; if we get back to yesterday history, and we analyze the origins of WW1 and WWII, we will find that that war comes from an excess of the concentration of power put on few people and organizations hands, as related by many studies and many authors;

GERMANY and JAPON were an almost flagrant example of power concentration during WWI and II; from recent history, that was why steps were taken after the wars to ban this kind of power concentration where it could exist, political, ecumenical, and financial, and so on.

Today, we assist to an expansion of new models of power concentration, a new kind of need created and witch did not exist in the past, like the Internet and all needs invented around, to capture our attention in the beginning and become an addict of those virtual spaces witch invaded our lives and our family lives. GAFAM, BATX, BIG PHARMA are the most known examples; they manipulate us using many techniques like persuasion, brainwashing, NPL, profiling, influence, and so on; to get us into their grid-like spider.

To see the huge thing, try to shut down your home internet connection for just 24 hours, and you will see what happens;

nobody can live today without a connection to his or her social media.

Vaccines are today's example that explains BIG PHARMA power and virus manipulation to create and spread diseases; the government can use it as a new kind of biological war one.

From this perspective, this book comes to highlights these crucial topics and give readers a broad insight into what they face in day to day lives.

TODAY'S MONOPOLIES does not pretend to master any related topics but tried to give readers a broad picture of todays' facts and figure out its future.

TODAY'S MONOPOLIES tries to make it easier for you to understand all topics related to power concentration and the difficulties they faced, and its impact on the era in which they live.

Made in the USA
Middletown, DE
01 December 2021

53900734R00110